D0822677

Mark Pryce is Vicar of Smethwick Old Church, in the Diocese of Birmingham, England. Born and brought up in the Welsh Marches, he read English at the University of Sussex, and was previously Fellow and Dean of Chapel of Corpus Christi College, Cambridge. His previous publications include *Finding a Voice: Men, Women and the Community of the Church* and *Literary Companion to the Lectionary* (SPCK, 2001).

With thanksgiving for the life and ministry of

R. S. Thomas,
priest and poet:
true Word-bearer

Literary Companion
TO THE
Festivals

———◦———

A Poetic Gathering
to Accompany Liturgical Celebrations
of Commemorations and Festivals

Edited by

Mark Pryce

FORTRESS PRESS
Minneapolis

LITERARY COMPANION TO THE FESTIVALS

First Fortress Press edition 2003

Copyright © 2003 Mark Pryce

Published in collaboration with
the Society for Promoting Christian Knowledge, London.
All rights reserved.
Except for brief quotations in critical articles or reviews,
no part of this book may be reproduced in any manner
without prior written permission from the publisher.
Write to: Permissions, Augsburg Fortress, Box 1209, Minneapolis, MN 55440.

Scripture quotations are from the New Revised Standard Version of the Bible,
copyright © 1989 by the Division of Christian Education of the
National Council of Churches of Christ in the USA. Used by permission.
All rights reserved.

Cover design: Monica Capoferri
Cover graphic: "Canticum Canticorum" by Eric Gill
Book design and typesetting: Kenneth Burnley, Wirral, Cheshire

ISBN 0-8006-3605-8

Manufactured in Great Britain

06 05 04 03   1 2 3 4 5 6 7 8 9

Contents

Commemorations marked with an asterisk* are observed in the Calendar of Common Worship 2000 only.

Italicized Commemorations are observed in the Calendar of the *Lutheran Book of Worship* 1978 only.

Where Commemorations are included in both calendars, but observed on different dates, the earlier date in the year is given, with the alternative in square brackets [CW] or [LBW].

Entries in **bold type** indicate Festivals.

FOREWORD

Mark Pryce now offers a second volume of resources to fund the faith, imagination, and liturgical practices of the Church. This volume, a sequel to *Literary Companion to the Lectionary*, brings together samples of literary articulation by and about 'the saints of the Church', reaching back to the early centuries of the Church and extending into its contemporary life. The readings are arranged through the calendar year to mark selected 'saint days' as they appear, with a brief introduction for each piece which connects it with a particular saint or group of witnesses. It is clear that these resources can be used in the corporate life of the congregation as well as in more personal practices of piety and devotion.

In helping us to recognize the saints afresh – some better known, some less well known – this book suggests a 'thickening' of the memory of the Church and an appreciation of the present communion of the Church that takes place before a 'great cloud of witnesses'. In my own reading of these pages it occurred to me that in a time of secularization and amnesia, the great fellowship of saints that funds the present Church merits the particular attention and greater appreciation which Mark Pryce offers us here. I have run across three characterizations of the saints that strike me as peculiarly poignant to this volume:

1   Saints are those women and men of faith through whose faces and lives 'the light comes'. It is the light of divine presence acted in human obedience, a light in the midst of the characteristic darknesses of fear, anxiety, brutality and all of the derivative pathologies that are so powerful among us. The Church intuitively gathers around such 'windows' of divine presence.
2   Saints are those who know the primal language of 'the other'. The 'other' in the first instance is God; saints are the ones who cede their energy and attention beyond themselves to focus on God who is profoundly other. As a consequence, the mood of the articulations in this book is characteristically one of praise. But without self-preoccupation, the othering of the saints pertains to brothers and sisters as well, the day-to-day others who bespeak the generous, gracious rule of God.

3   Saints are those who find themselves in the presence of the 'smell of death' and who abide in that place. All the rest of us leave as soon as possible, and depart for safer places. But since these beloved are not preoccupied with their own safety, they linger in the unsafe places to commit acts of healing solidarity.

It is easy and obvious to notice that by these markings, saints commit daily acts of subversion,

- to counter the darkness of despair,
- to counter the fear of the other, and
- to counter flight from the stench of death.

What a difference this communion of these saints makes!

In this book Mark Pryce not only names and appreciates the saints. He mediates to us their utterances. What this collection evidences is that the 'mother tongue' of saints is characteristically *poetry*, a kind of open, elusive attachment to the Mystery that resists flattening prose. The outcome of such poetry from the hands of such peculiar people is an endless porousness that permits easy access between the mystery of God and the reality of the world. Thus the poetry of Richard Ntiru, given for the commemoration of Janani Luwum, Ugandan Martyr in 1977, contrasts 'us' with the world:

> If it is true
> > that the world talks too much ...
> > that the world sees too much ...
> > that the world hears too much ...
> > that the world moves too much ...
> then let's all keep quiet ...
> > let's all close our eyes ...
> > let's wax our ears ...
> > let's stand statuestill ...
> for the dumb don't tell lies
> for the blind can't be peeping-toms
> for the deaf cannot eavesdrop
> for the crippled can't trespass.
> > > (pp. 19–20)

In applying these words of the Ugandan poet to the courageous witness of the Ugandan archbishop, Mark reveals how both poet and martyr outline in a quite concrete way a refusal of the world.

Robert Bridges affirms the cruciality of praise:

> Man doeth nothing well, be it great or small,
> Save to praise God; but that hath saved all.
>
> (p. 44)

All that counts is praise!

Christina Rossetti (1894) finds, along with all the saints, God to be a place of measureless well-being that provides buoyancy for life:

> Yea, Thou the measureless ocean for my rill:
> Seeking I find, and finding, seek Thee still.
>
> (p. 48)

Saints are those who refuse despair. Rossetti's lines chosen for the commemoration of Gregory the Great (604) direct us towards the saints as those who put voice to and life down in *hope*:

> A life of hope deferred too often is
> A life of wasted opportunities;
> A life of perished hope too often is
> A life of all-lost opportunities:
> Yet hope is but the flower and not the root,
> And hope is still the flower and not the fruit; –
> Arise and sow and weed: a day shall come
> When also thou shalt keep thy harvest home.
>
> (p. 116)

And the words of Scheffler, translated by John Wesley, in commemorating Luther and all the great saints and martyrs of the Reformation, voice *love* for God above and beyond all else:

> Thee will I love, my strength, my tower;
> Thee will I love, my joy, my crown;
> Thee will I love with all my power,
> In all my works, and thee alone!

Thee will I love till the pure fire
Fill my whole soul with chaste desire.

(p. 139)

And to love he adds his *thanks*:

> I thank thee, Uncreated Sun,
>   That thy bright beams on me have shined;
> I thank thee, who hast overthrown
>   My foes, and heal'd my wounded mind;
> I thank thee, whose enlivening voice
> Bids my free heart in thee rejoice.

(p. 140)

These articulations are typical of the world of lyric offered in this book, all verses that are acts of resistance against a God-emptied world made lean and flat, a world too soon in despair. The saints are people who live and trust and rejoice otherwise. These words are images of another world palpably present here and now.

What an offer . . . *saints* in *poetry*, refusing what is prosaic and without spirit. These resources are an offer now for a Church that can be in mission to counter a world of death. These best human windows of translucence attest to an alternative. Mark Pryce focuses on an ordering that is particularly familiar among Anglicans and Lutherans. But for Christian worshippers across the ecumenical spectrum, these resources are rich and powerful. This collection counters our *individualism* by the thickness of this community of utterance. This collection counters *amnesia* with rich remembering. This collection counters *profanation* with unembarrassed holiness. With these voices of *community*, *remembering* and *holiness*, the world is made different. Thus, dear reader, welcome to these vehicles of newness, a most happy offer!

WALTER BRUEGGEMANN
Columbia Theological Seminary
11 November 2002

INTRODUCTION

Most religious traditions share a sense of time in which certain periods are marked out with special significance. In this way the passage of days, weeks and years may come to carry a spiritual meaning. The liturgical year of the Christian Church has been arranged to set before us the principal events of the Saviour's life, and woven around these key celebrations of God revealed in Jesus Christ are the festivals of the Blessed Virgin Mary, the Apostles and saints, and commemorations of holy men and holy women through the ages, whose lives have been transformed by his Spirit and reveal his grace. Anglicans and Lutherans share this same liturgical pattern of the great Christian festivals and the commemoration of saints whom both churches hold in a common esteem. In addition, English-speaking Anglicans and Lutherans share a common literary heritage which embraces hymnody, prayer and the language of the Bible. The aim of this book is to enrich our common celebration of the liturgical year through offering poems and prose for particular festivals and commemorations. Through sharing in these words we shall deepen prayer, stimulate reflection and strengthen our spiritual friendship in Christ, within the communion of saints.

In focusing on saints' days this anthology is a partner volume to *Literary Companion to the Lectionary*, which gives material for Sundays and Principal Feasts. The large number of saints' days in the Calendar means that to have included them all would be beyond the scope of a single book of this kind. A selection has been made largely on the basis of commemorations which are common to both Anglican and Lutheran traditions, or where a literary reference seems to suggest a mutual sympathy. Those which occur only in the Calendar of Common Worship 2000 or the *Lutheran Book of Worship* 1978 are clearly indicated. The hope is that these pages offer a kind of literary ecumenism, as well as opening our eyes to the holiness of the whole Church: catholic, apostolic, reformed.

Christians acknowledge that it was through the Word that all things came into being. In Jesus Christ, Word-among-us, all created things find their true meaning, and ultimately their fulfilment. The Creator's self-expression in and through the Word becomes the language which creates, sustains and completes our world, and God the Spirit draws out from us our words in response. Language then, including its literary forms and complex word structures, is God-born and God-bearing. As those who have beheld the glory, the grace and truth of God spoken in Christ, the Church embraces literary forms and cherishes words as the language given for praise and proclamation, as the continuing activity of the creating, communicating Spirit of God active within us and between us. We need not shy away from the possibilities of literature, nor stifle the wonders of our literary inheritance as Christians, as we do too often now for fear of its strangeness. Glutted as we are with the alluring entertainment of television, Christians are alienated from our own literary tradition – though the skill and brilliance of contemporary religious poets and writers reveal that this tradition is still vibrant even if it is on the margins of the mainstream Churches.

For just as the Calendar of holy days gives us the opportunity to celebrate saints of every age and culture, and to move beyond the experience of the immediate and familiar, so this is intended to be an anthology of diverse pieces, and has a particular purpose of bringing out the 'old' as well as the 'new' from the literary treasury. From the earliest centuries of the Church, building upon the Hebrew psalms and the Scriptures, words have been shaped into the forms of hymns and poems to express praise and wonder as the faithful contemplate the glory and the mystery of God. These writings are for us too as people of words, the community formed by the Word. Indeed, our Christian Calendar is itself a kind of poem, a structuring of time into a lived shape of sacred meaning, with all the nuances of inter-relationship and the genesis of fresh, unexpected insight to which formal expression gives rise. In the keeping of festivals the Church is engaging in a creative act with days, living out her corporate life in a process of making with memory, significance and occasion just as drama, poetry and literature do. This calendrical flow of celebration, bearing along the saints and martyrs and inspirers of the Church, is a narration in time of salvation in Christ, an expression of redemption in the lives of successive generations and diverse cultures, a dramatic story-poem to be lived and prayed. It inspires, renews, challenges, integrates and so expands our spiritual vision through the very participation it stimulates and sustains. Enjoy!

I am grateful to all those who have helped me in assembling this *Companion*, and especially to Leslie Houlden, Ruth McCurry and James Woodward.

MARK PRYCE

ST GREGORY OF NAZIANZUS*

BISHOP AND POET, 389

——◄◦►——

Hymn to God

Translated from the Greek of Gregory of Nazianzus
by John McGuckin

Though Gregory's contribution to the theological understanding and
doctrinal expression of the fourth-century Church was fundamental, he
loathed the controversy and intrigue of ecclesiastical politics (in which
his friend Basil involved him by consecrating him as Bishop). Through his
role in preaching and teaching Trinitarian doctrine, Gregory was elected
Patriarch of Constantinople, but resigned in 381 to live in seclusion at his
family home near Nazianzus. There he gave himself over to prayer and the
writing of poetry in which his profound theological insights are given
voice in a context of praise.

You are above all things
and what other way can we rightly sing of you?

How can words sing your praise
When no word can speak of you?
How can the mind consider you
When no mind can ever grasp you?
You alone are unutterable
From the time you created all things that can be spoken of.
You alone are unknowable
From the time you created all things that can be known.
All things cry out about you
    Those which speak, and those which cannot speak,
All things honour you
    Those which think, and those which cannot think.
For there is one longing, one groaning, that all things have
    for you.

1

All things pray to you that comprehend your plan
And offer you a silent hymn.
In you, the One, all things abide
And all things endlessly run to you
Who are the end of all.
And you are the One, and All, and none of them –
Being not one thing, not all things.
You who bear all names
How shall I name you, who cannot be named?
What heavenly mind can penetrate those veils above the
    clouds?

Be merciful
You who are greater than all things
For what other way can we rightly sing of you?

St Kentigern (Mungo)*

BISHOP AND MISSIONARY, 603

————◄◊►————

Soul-Shrine

Ann MacDonald, Scottish, nineteenth century

Kentigern's missionary journeys ranged from Scotland to Cumbria and into Wales, and so here is a Scottish poem-prayer for safety in travel.

> Thou angel of God who hast charge of me
> From the fragrant Father of mercifulness,
> The gentle encompassing of the Sacred Heart
> To make round my soul-shrine this night,
>   Oh, round my soul-shrine this night.
>
> Ward from me every distress and danger,
> Encompass my course over the ocean of truth,
> I pray thee, place thy pure light before me
> O bright beauteous angel on this very night,
>   Bright beauteous angel on this very night.
>
> Be Thyself the guiding star above me,
> Illume Thou to me every reef and shoal,
> Pilot my barque on the crest of the wave,
> To the restful haven of the waveless sea,
>   Oh, the restful haven of the waveless sea.

MARTIN LUTHER KING JNR

RENEWER OF SOCIETY AND MARTYR, 1968

————◄◦►————

From *Transformed Nonconformist*

Martin Luther King Jnr, American, 1929–68

Martin Luther King published a selection of his sermons in 1963 in a collection called *Strength to Love*, in response to national and international demand to share in the vision of social justice and racial equality which he expressed so eloquently, and for which he campaigned so powerfully. Even so, he writes modestly in his introduction that sermons are to be heard as discourse rather than read as texts. The following year King was awarded the Nobel Peace Prize. The poet whom he quotes, James Russell Lowell (1819–91), was American Minister in England from 1880 to 1885, and among his work are memorial odes written after the Civil War.

Nowhere is the tragic tendency to conform more evident than in the church, an institution which has often served to crystallize, conserve, and even bless the patterns of majority opinion. The erstwhile sanction by the church of slavery, racial segregation, war, and economic exploitation is testimony to the fact that the church has hearkened more to the authority of the world than to the authority of God. Called to be the moral guardian of the community, the church has at times preserved that which is immoral and unethical. Called to combat social evils, it has remained silent behind stained-glass windows. Called to lead men on the highway of brotherhood and to summon them to rise above the narrow confines of race and class, it has enunciated and practised racial exclusiveness.

We preachers have also been tempted by the enticing cult of conformity . . . We preach comforting sermons and avoid saying anything from our pulpit which might disturb the respectable views of the comfortable members of our congregations. Have we ministers of Jesus Christ sacrificed truth on the altar of self-interest and, like Pilate, yielded our convictions to the demands of the crowd?

We need to recapture the gospel glow of the early Christians, who were nonconformists in the truest sense of the word and refused to shape their witness according to the mundane patterns of the world. Willingly they sacrificed fame, fortune, and life itself in behalf of a cause they knew to be right. Quantitatively small, they were qualitatively giants. Their powerful gospel put an end to such barbaric evils as infanticide and bloody gladiatorial contests. Finally, they captured the Roman Empire for Jesus Christ.

The hope of a secure and livable world lies with the disciplined nonconformists, who are dedicated to justice, peace, and brotherhood. The trailblazers in human, academic, scientific and religious freedom have always been nonconformists. In any cause that concerns the progress of mankind, put your faith in the nonconformist!

In his essay 'Self Reliance' Emerson wrote, 'Whoso would be a man must be a nonconformist.' The Apostle Paul reminds us that whoso would be a Christian must also be a nonconformist. Any Christian who blindly accepts the opinions of the majority and in fear and timidity follows a path of expediency and social approval is a mental and spiritual slave. Mark well these words from the pen of James Russell Lowell:

> They are slaves who fear to speak
> For the fallen and the weak;
> They are slaves who will not choose
> Hatred, scoffing, and abuse,
> Rather than in silence shrink
> From the truth they needs must think;
> They are slaves who dare not be
> In the right with two or three.

5

18 January

THE CONFESSION OF ST PETER
THE WEEK OF PRAYER FOR CHRISTIAN UNITY BEGINS

————◁◦▷————

St Peter

Christina Rossetti, English, 1830–94

In recalling how Simon Peter, 'the Rock', not only confessed Jesus as Christ but also resisted and denied him, Rossetti's sonnet meditates on our own great need for Christ's forgiveness, cleansing and love.

> St Peter once: 'Lord, dost Thou wash my feet?' –
> Much more I say: 'Lord, dost Thou stand and knock
> At my closed heart more rugged than a rock,
> Bolted and barred, for Thy soft touch unmeet,
> Nor garnished nor in any wise made sweet?'
> Owls roost within and dancing satyrs mock.
> Lord, I have heard the crowing of the cock
> And have not wept: ah, Lord, thou knowest it.
> Yet still I hear Thee knocking, still I hear:
> 'Open to Me, look on Me eye to eye,
> That I may wring thy heart and make it whole;
> And teach thee love because I hold thee dear
> And sup with thee in gladness soul with soul,
> And sup with thee in glory by and by.'

RICHARD ROLLE OF HAMPOLE*

MYSTIC AND POET, 1349

———◄◦►———

Prayer before, during and after food

From *The Form of Living*, Chapter 7, by Richard Rolle,
English, *c.*1290–1349, translated by Mark Pryce

Rolle is the first great English mystic of whom we have any definite
knowledge, and the first to write in English, not only in prose but in verse.
A layman and hermit, Rolle teaches that contemplative prayer is like song:
'Song I call it when in a soul the sweetness of everlasting praise is received
with plenteous burning, and thought is turned into song; the mind is
changed into full sweet sound.' Though scholars dispute its original
authorship, Rolle gives this lyric in his *The Form of Living* as a personal
love-song to be said privately during a meal, so that God may be praised in
the mind with every mouthful of food.

> Praised be thou, O King,
> and thanked be thou, O King,
> and blessed be thou, O King,
>   O Jesu, all my joying,
> of all thy gifts, (thyself) most good;
> who for me spilled thy blood,
> and died upon the rood;
>   O give me grace to sing
>   the song of thy praising.

THE CONVERSION OF ST PAUL

THE WEEK OF PRAYER FOR CHRISTIAN UNITY CLOSES

———◄◦►———

Sonnet *On His Blindness*

John Milton, English, 1608–74

In celebrating the dynamic, missionary apostolate of St Paul, we recall the three dark days of his blindness in Damascus, during which the inner light dawned and his conversion to Christ began (Acts 9.3ff.). For Paul, the loss of status, troubles and imprisonment which resulted is always outweighed by the supreme value of knowing and serving Christ (Philippians 3:7ff.; 2 Corinthians 6.4–10). Milton's sonnet, written soon after he went totally blind in 1652, speaks eloquently of serving Christ with patience in all circumstances, even those of great difficulty.

> When I consider how my light is spent
>   Ere half my days in this dark world and wide,
>   And that one talent which is death to hide
> Lodged with me useless, though my soul more bent
> To serve therewith my maker, and present
>   My true account, lest he returning chide,
>   'Doth God exact day-labour, light denied?'
>   I fondly ask. But Patience, to prevent
> That murmur, soon replies, 'God doth not need
>   Either man's work or his own gifts; who best
>   Bear his mild yoke, they serve him best: his state
> Is kingly. Thousands at his bidding speed,
>   And post o'er land and ocean without rest;
>   They also serve who only stand and wait.'

26 January

ST TIMOTHY AND ST TITUS
[AND SILAS]
COMPANIONS OF ST PAUL

——◄◦►——

Visitor

Les Murray, Australian, 1932–

Timothy, Titus and Silas were partners in Paul's mission and accompanied him in some of the hazards and contentions of the evangelical task. This brief poem (printed here in its entirety!) sums up the risk and exposure which is experienced by 'the one who comes'.

> He knocks at the door
> And listens to his heart approaching.

LYDIA, DORCAS AND PHOEBE

DISCIPLES

——◄◦►——

He Wishes for the Cloths of Heaven

W. B. Yeats, Irish, 1865–1939

Yeats' exquisite poem about the vulnerability of dreams suggests something of the vision of service and love of neighbour which inspired these women of the early Church to make present heavenly realities in the life of the first Christian communities. Lydia, a dealer in purple cloth (Acts 16.11ff.), was one of Paul's first converts in Philippi, and she became a leader and mainstay of the church there. Phoebe, a benefactor and Deacon of the church at Cenchreae, was specially commended by Paul to the church in Rome because of her ministry (Romans 16.1ff.). Dorcas, called Tabitha in Aramaic, made clothing for members of the church in Joppa and was celebrated for her good works and acts of charity (Acts 9.36ff.).

Had I the heavens' embroidered cloths,
Enwrought with golden and silver light,
The blue and the dim and the dark cloths
Of night and light and the half-light,
I would spread the cloths under your feet:
But I, being poor, have only my dreams;
I have spread my dreams under your feet;
Tread softly because you tread on my dreams.

28 January [LBW 7 March]

St Thomas Aquinas

PRIEST, PHILOSOPHER AND HYMN WRITER,
1274

————◄◦►————

From *The Selected Letters of Edith Sitwell* (1970)

English, 1887–1964

Dame Edith Sitwell was received into the Roman Catholic Church in August 1955, and read the writings of Aquinas as part of her instruction (though she had encountered his work at an earlier stage through the devout Anglican poet and publisher Charles Williams). This letter, written from the Sitwell home in Italy to her spiritual adviser, demonstrates how Aquinas' thought stimulated Dame Edith's own insights and inspired her in making further connections.

To Father Philip Caraman

3 June 1955
Castello di Montegufoni

Dear Father Caraman,

I cannot express to you my gratitude for having recommended these books to me. The first feeling they give me is one of absolute certainty. They – and especially the wonderful writings of St Thomas Aquinas . . . , make one see doubt – perhaps I am not expressing this properly – as a complete failure of intellect. Then again I see that purely intellectual belief is not enough: one must not only *think* one is believing, but *know* one is believing. There has to be a sixth sense in faith . . .

When I was a very small child, I began to see the patterns of the world, the images of wonder. And I asked myself why those patterns should be repeated – the feather and the fern and the rose and the acorn in the patterns of frost on the window – pattern after pattern repeated again and again. And even then I knew that this was telling us something. I founded my poetry upon it. Did

11

you, I wonder, know Dr Hubble, of the Expanding Universe – one of the greatest men I ever knew. One day, in California, he showed me signs of universes unseen by the naked eye, and millions of light-years away. I said to him 'How terrifying!' 'Only when you are not used to them,' he replied. 'When you *are* used to them, they are comforting. For then you know there is nothing to worry about – nothing at all!'

That was a few months before he died. And I suppose now that he knows how truly he spoke. I was most deeply moved by that. I could never cease to be so.

With my deep gratitude,

Yours very sincerely,

Edith Sitwell.

This is a most inadequate letter. For some reason I cannot express myself in the slightest at present.

1 February

ST BRIGID*

ABBESS OF KILDARE, c.525

———◄◦►———

Bride the Aid-Woman

From the *Carmina Gadelica* (1900), collected and translated from
the Gaelic by Alexander Carmichael, Scottish, 1832–1912

Though little is known for certain about St Brigid, also called St Bride, she
has been regarded with great veneration in Ireland. In Celtic lore Brigid
presides over beauty, fire and art. She is the beautiful sister and helper of
Mary and the foster-mother of Jesus, and the seventh-century poem
'Fothairt' refers to her as a 'second Mary, mother of the great Lord'.
Through her is expressed the Celtic sense of participation in the mystery
of the birth of Jesus.

There came to me assistance,
Mary fair and Bride;
As Anna bore Mary,
As Mary bore Christ,
As Eile bore John the Baptist
Without flaw in him,
Aid thou me in mine unbearing,
 Aid me, O Bride!

As Christ was conceived of Mary
Full perfect on every hand,
Assist thou me, foster-mother,
The conception to bring from the bone;
And as thou didst aid the Virgin of joy,
Without gold, without corn, without kine,
Aid thou me, great is my sickness,
 Aid me, O Bride.

Eile – Elizabeth; *kine* – cattle/cows.

13

ANSKAR (ANSGAR)

ARCHBISHOP OF HAMBURG, AND MISSIONARY TO DENMARK AND SWEDEN, 865

————◄◦►————

From *The Children of the Lord's Supper*

Translated from the Swedish of Esaias Tegner by
Henry W. Longfellow, American, 1807–82

A native of Picardy, Anskar's missionary work was widespread: in Sweden, where he built the first Christian church, Denmark and Germany. In this Swedish poem a wise teacher enlightens the faithful who are gathered to hear him and to partake in the Lord's Supper.

> Prayer is Innocence' friend; and willingly flieth incessant
> 'Twixt the earth and the sky, the carrier-pigeon of heaven.
> Son of Eternity, fettered in Time, and an exile, the Spirit
> Tugs at his chains evermore, and struggles like flame ever
>   upward.
> Still he recalls with emotion his Father's manifold mansions,
> Thinks of the land of his fathers, where blossomed more
>   freely the flowerets,
> Shone a more beautiful sun, and he played with the wingèd angels.
> Then grows the earth too narrow, too close; and homesick for
>   heaven
> Longs the wanderer again; and the Spirit's longings are worship;
> Worship is called his most beautiful hour, and its tongue is
>   entreaty.
> Ah! when the infinite burden of life descendeth upon us,
> Crushes to earth our hope, and, under the earth, in the graveyard,
> Then it is good to pray unto God; for His sorrowing children
> Turns He ne'er from His door, but He heals and helps and
>   consoles them.

5 February

THE MARTYRS OF JAPAN

1597

———◄○►———

From *A Life of Jesus* (1973)

Shusaku Endo, Japanese, 1923– , translated by
Richard A. Schuchert SJ

As Japan's foremost Christian writer, Endo's fiction is known internation-
ally, and especially his controversial novel *Silence* (1969), set in the brutal
persecution of seventeenth-century Japan. In the last chapter of his *Life of
Jesus*, Endo reflects as a novelist on the character of the disciples as depicted
in the books of the New Testament. He wonders what brought about the
mysterious transformation in the disciples, from uncomprehending and
cowardly individuals who abandon Jesus in his weakness, into a body of
Apostles, full of conviction and understanding. It is the power of Christ
crucified and raised, he concludes – a power made perfect in human
weakness, an enduring power which enables the martyrs of all ages and
cultures to bear witness in their living and their dying.

The psychology of the disciples as I have stated the case, is not
explicit in the New Testament, but between the lines we cannot
escape the feel of it. Even I as a solitary novelist in the Orient can
sense that much . . .

The carpenter who grew up in the back country of a weak
nation was in his brief career an other-worldly sort of teacher
whom in the end not even his own disciples could appreciate. Not
until after his death were they able to grasp what kind of person he
really was. For all I know, there may well be an analogy here
between their inability to understand Jesus during his lifetime and
our own inability to understand the whole mystery of human life.
For Jesus represents all humanity. Furthermore, just as we, while we
live in this world, cannot understand the ways of God, so Jesus

himself was inscrutable for the disciples. His whole life embraced the simplicity of living only for love, and because he lived for love alone, in the eyes of the disciples he seemed to be ineffectual. His death was required before the disciples could raise the veil and see into what lay hidden behind the weakness.

THOMAS BRAY*

PRIEST, EDUCATIONALIST AND MISSIONARY, 1730

———◄◦►———

The Meaning of Existence

Les Murray, Australian, 1932–

Founder of two great Anglican missionary societies, the Society for Promoting Christian Knowledge and the Society for the Propagation of the Gospel (now the United Society), as the Bishop of London's Commissary in the American colony of Maryland from 1696 onwards, Bray was instrumental in strengthening the Anglican Church in America and developing its life and mission. In his pamphlets, such as *The Layman's Library* (*c.*1700), Bray put forward a scheme for the theological and general education of both laity and clergy in America through an integral network of lending libraries for parish, deanery, province and, at 'general' level, together with free schools, the preparation of prospective 'native clergymen' for service in the colonies, and the establishment of a Suffragan Bishop in Maryland. Though much of what he had proposed never came to pass in his lifetime, Bray was successful in raising funds and sending collections of books to parishes in New York, North Carolina, Rhode Island, Jamaica and elsewhere, as well as to Maryland. In this sense Bray is credited as the founder of the American Public Library System. In continuing Christian mission in a postmodern world very different from Bray's, agencies such as SPCK and USPG wrestle with many issues, not least relative notions of identity, truth and rationality, with a yearning for bodily and environmental integration, to which Murray's evocative poem alludes.

> Everything except language
> knows the meaning of existence.
> Trees, planets, rivers, time
> know nothing else. They express it
> moment by moment as the universe.

Even this fool of a body
lives it in part, and would
have full dignity within it
but for the ignorant freedom
of my talking mind.

17 February

JANANI LUWUM*

ARCHBISHOP OF UGANDA, AND MARTYR, 1977

———◄◦►———

If it is true

Richard Ntiru, Ugandan, 1946–

As Anglican Archbishop of Uganda, Janani Luwum made a courageous and heroic stand against the oppression and injustice of the Amin regime. He was assassinated in an automobile 'accident' most probably arranged by government agents. These words by a Ugandan poet who lived through the same period of terror celebrate the values of contemplation, honesty and stability. The last lines recall the radical demands of the Gospel (Matthew 18.8–9).

If it is true
that the world talks too much
then let's all keep quiet
and hear the eloquence
of silence

If it is true
that the world sees too much
then let's all close our eyes
and see the inner vision
beneath the closed eyes

If it is true
that the world hears too much
then let's wax our ears
and listen to the chastity of inner music
that defies the betrayal
by the wayward wind

If it is true
that the world moves too much
then let's stand statuestill
and imitate the stubborn will
of trees
that move without being peripatetic

for the dumb don't tell lies

for the blind can't be peeping-toms

for the deaf cannot eavesdrop

for the crippled can't trespass.

MARTIN LUTHER

RENEWER OF THE CHURCH AND
HYMN WRITER, 1546

———◄○►———

From deepest woe I cry to thee

Translated from the German of Martin Luther, 1483–1546,
by Catherine Winkworth, English, 1827–78

In this hymn, written as a congregational version of Psalm 130, Luther
sums up his theology of grace beautifully, and with great pastoral reassurance.

> From deepest woe I cry to thee;
> Lord, hear me, I implore thee!
> Bend down thy gracious ear to me;
> I lay my sins before thee.
> If thou rememberest every sin,
> if nought but just reward we win,
> could we abide thy presence?
>
> Thou grantest pardon through thy love;
> thy grace alone availeth.
> Our works could ne'er our guilt remove;
> yea, e'en the best life faileth.
> For none may boast themselves of aught,
> but must confess thy grace hath wrought
> whate'er in them is worthy.
>
> And thus my hope is in the Lord,
> and not in my own merit;
> I rest upon his faithful word
> to them of contrite spirit.
> That he is merciful and just,
> here is my comfort and my trust;
> his help I wait with patience.

St Matthias

APOSTLE

————◁◦▷————

From *Barchester Towers* (1857), Volume I, Chapter 6

Anthony Trollope, English, 1815–82

Recalling that Matthias was chosen to take the place of Judas, the Apostle who betrayed Jesus (Acts 1.15ff.), the collect for the day prays that the Church might be taught and led by faithful pastors. In his 'Barsetshire' novels Trollope makes an acute study of power-play and ambition in the Church of his time – indeed, perhaps the Church of any period. The epitome of the insincere but opinionated clergyman is Obadiah Slope, domestic chaplain to the Bishop of Barchester. Here, after reporting the odiousness of a sermon with which Slope makes his debut in the cathedral, the narrator laments the overbearing, insincere and tedious sermonizing of the clergy.

There is, perhaps, no greater hardship at present inflicted on mankind in civilized and free countries, than the necessity of listening to sermons. No one but a preaching clergyman has, in these realms, the power of compelling an audience to sit silent, and be tormented. No one but a preaching clergyman can revel in platitudes, truisms, and untruisms, and yet receive, as his undisputed privilege, the same respectful demeanour as though words of impassioned eloquence, or persuasive logic, fell from his lips. Let a professor of law or physic find his place in a lecture-room, and there pour forth jejune words and useless empty phrases, and he will pour them forth to empty benches. Let a barrister attempt to talk without talking well, and he will talk but seldom. A judge's charge need be listened to perforce by none but the jury, prisoner, and gaoler. A Member of Parliament can be coughed down or counted out. Town-councillors can be tabooed. But no-one can rid himself of the preaching clergyman. He is the bore of the age, the old man whom we Sinbads cannot shake off, the nightmare that disturbs our

Sunday's rest, the incubus that overloads our religion and makes God's service distasteful. We are not forced into Church! No: but we desire more than that. We desire not to be forced to stay away. We desire, nay, we are resolute, to enjoy the comfort of public worship; but we desire also that we may do so without an amount of tedium which ordinary human nature cannot endure with patience; that we may be able to leave the house of God without the anxious longing for escape, which is the common consequence of common sermons.

whom we Sinbads . . . – a reference to the character Sinbad the Sailor from *The Arabian Nights* who is burdened with an old man on his back who cannot be shaken off.

GEORGE HERBERT

PRIEST AND POET, 1633

———◄◌►———

Prayer

George Herbert, Anglo-Welsh, 1593–1633

Herbert's poetry is unsurpassed as an expression of the experience of prayer and relationship with God, both its exquisite pleasure and its darker sides. Here he celebrates prayer as a manifold blessing which is corporate yet intimate, grounded yet mystical.

> Prayer the Church's banquet, Angels' age,
>   God's breath in man returning to his birth,
>   The soul in paraphrase, heart in pilgrimage,
> The Christian plummet sounding heav'n and earth;
> Engine against th' Almighty, sinners' tower,
>   Reversed thunder, Christ-side-piercing spear,
>   The six-days-world transposing in an hour,
> A kind of tune, which all things hear and fear;
> Softness, and peace, and joy, and love, and bliss,
>   Exalted Manna, gladness of the best,
>   Heaven in ordinary, man well drest,
> The milky way, the bird of Paradise,
>   Church-bells beyond the stars heard, the soul's blood,
>   The land of spices; something understood.

St David*

BISHOP AND PATRON OF WALES, c.601

—◄◦►—

From *Saint David's Last Sermon*

Translated from the Welsh of Saunders Lewis, 1893–1984,
by Joseph P. Clancy

This poem by the left-wing, Welsh Nationalist, Roman Catholic writer
Saunders Lewis links the gentle teaching of St David – in contrast to his
reputation as a demanding, aristocratic leader – with 'the little way' of
humble Thérèse of Lisieux and Bernadette of Lourdes. The spirituality of
love which David commended, and which the ordinary people of Wales
have remembered, continues through history to the present day, across
divisions of class, nationality and gender.

> Strange, the sermon that David preached
> After mass, the Sunday before the first of March,
> To the crowd that had come there to grieve for his dying:
> 'Brothers and sisters, be cheerful,
> Keep the faith, and do the little things
> You have seen and heard from me.
> As for me, I will go the road our fathers went.
> Fare you well,' David said,
> 'And never, henceforth, shall we see one another.'
>
> . . . no miracle, no angel, were found in David's sermon
> After mass, the Sunday before the first of March,
> For the crowd who had come there to grieve for his dying,
> No summoning of the cloister as witness to the glories;
> But an urging to the lowly paths: Be cheerful
> And keep the faith and do the little things
> You have seen and heard from me.

It has been a fearful thing to historians, the rule of David,
With the Egyptian whip of his abstinence and the heavy
    yoke,
Lord of the saints, great-grandson of Cunedda and the
    purple.
But his final words, the sermon that nested in the memory
Of those who prayed on Teifi's banks through centuries
Of terror, through war, beneath the frown of the vulture-
    like castles,
Through the ages when the grasshopper was a burden,
They were maidenly words, a nun's tenderness,
'The little way' of Theresa to the purification and the
    union,
And the way of the poor lass who saw Mary at Lourdes.

JOHN AND CHARLES WESLEY

EVANGELISTS AND HYMN WRITERS, 1791 AND 1788

————◄◦►————

Sustained by the practical, affective spirituality and interconnecting church fellowship which the Wesley brothers developed, their preaching and teaching began a revival in English Christianity which quickly extended to North America, and which became established as a distinct and vital Christian denomination throughout the world. Fundamental to Methodism from the outset has been its hymnody, which began in the emphasis Charles and John gave to the language and music of praise. Their hymns are outstanding expressions of Christian devotion, steeped as they are in scriptural imagery and grounded in both traditional theology and personal experience. The hymns draw deep from a range of spiritualities across languages and historical periods, exemplified in Charles' breadth of vision, and by John's beautiful translations of hymns from the German seventeenth century (see entry for Reformation Day). In his Preface to Charles Wesley's Hymnbook of 1780, John brings out the profound role of poetry in 'piety', that is, in the expression of Christian belief, devotion and practice. In Charles' hymn 'Thou Shepherd of Israel, and mine', we see the rich combination of scriptural image, sacramental devotion and mystical prayer which his hymns offer.

From the *Preface to the 1780 Hymnbook*

John Wesley, English, 1703–91

May I be permitted to add a few words with regard to the poetry? Then I will speak to those who are the judges thereof, with all freedom and unreserved. To these I may say, without offense: In all these hymns there is no doggerel, no botches, nothing put in to patch up the rhyme, no feeble expletives. Here is nothing turgid or bombast on the one hand, nor low or creeping on the other. Here are no *cant* expressions, no words without meaning. Those who impute this to us know not what they say. We talk common sense (whether they understand it or not) both in verse and prose, and use no word but in a fixed determinate sense. Here are (allow me to say) both the purity, the strength, and the elegance of the English language – and at the same time the utmost simplicity and plainness, suited to every capacity. Lastly, I desire men of taste to judge – these are the only competent judges – whether there is not in some of the following verses the true spirit of poetry, such as cannot be acquired by art and labour, but must be the gift of nature. By labour a man may become a tolerable imitator of Spenser, Shakespeare, or Milton, and may heap together pretty compound epithets, as 'pale-eyed', 'meek-eyed', and the like. But unless he is born a poet he will never attain the genuine *spirit of poetry* . . .

What is of infinitely more moment than the spirit of poetry is the spirit of piety. And I trust all persons of real judgement will find this breathing through the whole *Collection*. It is in this view chiefly that I would recommend it to every truly pious reader: as a means of raising or quickening the spirit of devotion, of confirming his faith, of enlivening his hope, and of increasing or kindling his love to God and man. When poetry thus keeps its place, as the handmaid of piety, it shall attain, not a poor perishable wreath, but a crown that fades not away.

Thou Shepherd of Israel, and mine

Charles Wesley, English, 1707–88

Thou Shepherd of Israel, and mine,
   The joy and desire of my heart,
For closer communion I pine,
   I long to reside where thou art:
The pasture I languish to find
   Where all, who their Shepherd obey,
Are fed, on thy bosom reclined,
   And screened from the heat of the day.

Ah! show me that happiest place,
   The place of thy people's abode,
Where saints in an ecstasy gaze,
   And hang on a crucified God;
Thy love for a sinner declare,
   Thy passion and death on the tree:
My spirit to Calvary bear,
   To suffer and triumph with thee.

'Tis there, with the lambs of thy flock,
   There only, I covet to rest,
To lie at the foot of the rock,
   Or rise to be hid in thy breast;
'Tis there I would always abide,
   And never a moment depart,
Concealed in the cleft of thy side,
   Eternally held in thy heart.

8 March

GEOFFREY STUDDERT KENNEDY*
PRIEST AND POET, 1929

———◄○►———

Waste

Geoffrey Studdert Kennedy, Irish, 1883–1929

Studdert Kennedy was a profoundly sensitive pastor who gained the trust
of British soldiers during the horrors and comradeship of World War I.
These experiences gave Studdert Kennedy the grounding for his theology
of a compassionate God so powerfully expressed in his poetry. This poem
is exceptionally stark, but it is the voice of one who has experienced the
realities of war first hand.

> Waste of Muscle, waste of Brain,
> Waste of Patience, waste of Pain,
> Waste of Manhood, waste of Health,
> Waste of Beauty, waste of Wealth,
> Waste of Blood, and waste of Tears,
> Waste of youth's most precious years,
> Waste of ways the saints have trod,
> Waste of Glory, waste of God, –
> War!

St Patrick

BISHOP, MISSIONARY AND PATRON OF
IRELAND, *c.460*

————◄◇►————

Paging St Patrick

Dorothy Parker, American, 1893–1967

There is no city on earth where the patron of the Irish is celebrated with more exuberance than in New York, where Dorothy Parker lived and worked, and centre of her literary circle, the Algonquin Round Table. Here she muses that Patrick, who is said to have expelled all the snakes from Ireland, would find many serpents awaiting him were he to visit her home town!

> The good Saint Patrick, in his day,
>   Performed a worthy act:
> He up and drove the snakes away,
>   With more technique than tact.
> Could he descend from realms above
>   And roam about New York,
> He'd find it reminiscent of
>   The good old days in Cork.
> The snakes he knew could never tie
>   The brand our village has –
> The kind that daily multiply
>   And thrive on tea and jazz.
>
> Should he his tales of snakes relate
>   We'd strive to hide a laugh;
> For, though the saint was wise and great,
>   He didn't know the half.
> Where'er he'd go, to dine or dance,
>   Or lunch, or tea, or sup,

The saint would have a splendid chance
    To do some cleaning up.
Could he but leave his present star,
    He'd see that things have changed –
How sad such little visits are
    Not easily arranged.

St Joseph of Nazareth
HUSBAND OF THE BLESSED VIRGIN MARY

———◁◇▷———

The Pay for Fosterage
Les Murray, Australian, 1932–

This poem pays tribute to Joseph's visionary faithfulness. For it was more than decency which dissuaded him from disgracing Mary or lapsing into bitterness: it was his obedience to God's plan of salvation revealed to him.

> The carpenter could have stayed
> Hunched over, at work on his chagrin,
> Left everything to the hush-ups
> And stone-evadings of women.
> He could have escaped the thousands
> Of years of speculation. The horns.
> But all that weakness was behind him.
> The courteous presence had spoken
> Unearthly sense to its equal,
> Himself. As he would be from now
> On into the world to come.

21 March

Thomas Cranmer

ARCHBISHOP OF CANTERBURY AND REFORMATION MARTYR, 1556

————◄◦►————

Concerning the Service of the Church

Thomas Cranmer, English, 1489–1556

The Preface to the Book of Common Prayer was written by Cranmer for the first Prayer Book of 1549, drawing heavily on other sources. The text continued in that introductory position, with minor amendments, through the 1552 revision, and into the 1662 version which was used by the early English-speaking Lutheran congregations in America. The brief Preface shows Cranmer's pastoral attitude to liturgy, and his acute attention to the power and accessibility of words.

There was never any thing by the wit of man so well devised, or so sure established, which in continuance of time hath not been corrupted: As, among other things, it may plainly appear by the Common Prayers in the Church, commonly called *Divine Service.* The first original and ground whereof if a man would search out by the ancient Fathers, he shall find, that the same was not ordained but of a good purpose, and for a great advancement of godliness. For they so ordered the matter, that the whole Bible (or the greatest part thereof) should be read over once every year; intending thereby, that the Clergy, and especially such as were Ministers in the congregation, should (by often reading, and meditation in God's word) be stirred up to godliness themselves, and be more able to exhort others by wholesome doctrine, and to confute them that were adversaries to the truth; and further, that the people, (by daily hearing of holy Scripture read in the Church) might continually profit more and more in the knowledge of God, and be more inflamed with the love of his true Religion.

But these many years passed, this godly and decent order of the ancient Fathers hath been so altered, broken, and neglected, by planting in uncertain Stories, and Legends, with multitude of Responds, Verses, vain Repetitions, Commemorations, and Synodals; that commonly when any Book of the Bible was begun, after three or four chapters were read out, all the rest were unread . . .

Yet, because there is no remedy, but that of necessity there must be some Rules; therefore certain Rules are here set forth; which, as they are few in number, so they are plain and easy to be understood. So that here you have an Order for Prayer, and for the reading of the holy Scripture, much agreeable to the mind and purpose of the old Fathers, and a great deal more profitable and commodious, than that which of late was used. It is more profitable, because here are left out many things, whereof some are untrue, some uncertain, some vain and superstitious; and nothing is ordained to be read, but the very pure Word of God, the holy Scriptures, or that which is agreeable to the same; and that in such Language and Order as is most easy and plain for the understanding both of the Readers and the Hearers. It is also more commodious, both for the shortness thereof, and for the plainness of the Order, and for that the Rules be few and easy.

JOHN DONNE

PRIEST AND POET, 1631

◄○►

Love's Growth

John Donne, English, 1572–1631

The richness and depth of Donne's religious imagination are rooted in the wealth of his life experience, much of it spent in London's élite society, where finally he became Dean of St Paul's Cathedral. He was brought up as a Roman Catholic, educated at Oxford (and possibly at Cambridge also), trained as a lawyer, became a gentleman adventurer at sea with the Earl of Essex and Walter Raleigh, joined an expedition to the Azores, was elected as a Member of Parliament, made a clandestine marriage, and earned a living through writing before he was ordained in the Church of England in mid-life. His celebrated sermons demonstrate a mastery of English language and a humane faith; his poetry is inspired by a spirituality which integrates the broad spectrum of human experience and understanding within the poetic vision – images from science, war, nature, sexual love, all cohere within the 'religious' to express, interrogate, enlighten. This 'secular' love poem is vibrant with the same exuberance which animates his 'sacred' verse.

> I scarce believe my love to be so pure
>   As I had thought it was,
>   Because it doth endure
> Vicissitude, and season, as the grass;
> Methinks I lied all winter, when I swore,
> My love was infinite, if spring make it more.
> But if this medicine, love, which cures all sorrow
> With more, not only be no quintessence,
> But mixed of all stuffs, paining soul, or sense,
> And of the sun his working vigour borrow,
> Love's not so pure, and abstract, as they use

To say, which have no mistress but their Muse,
But as all else, being elemented too,
Love sometimes would contemplate, sometimes do.

And yet not greater, but more eminent,
   Love by the spring is grown;
    As, in the firmament,
Stars by the sun are not enlarged, but shown,
Gentle love deeds, as blossoms on a bough,
From love's awakened root do bud out now.
If, as in water stirred more circles be
Produced by one, love such additions take,
Those like so many spheres, but one heaven make,
For, they are all concentric unto thee,
And though each spring do add to love new heat,
As princes do in times of action get
New taxes, and remit them not in peace,
No winter shall abate the spring's increase.

1 April

FREDERICK DENISON MAURICE*
PRIEST, NOVELIST AND TEACHER OF THE
FAITH, 1872

————◄○►————

Come, when no graver cares employ
Alfred, Lord Tennyson, English, 1809–92

With writers such as Charles Kingsley (*Alton Locke*, *The Water Babies*) and Thomas Hughes (*Tom Brown's Schooldays*), F. D. Maurice was one of the founders of English Christian Socialism. The apparent radicalism of his application of Christian principles to social reform, and the philosophical nature of his theology, met with considerable opposition. In 1853, Maurice's challenge to the popular conception of eternal punishment in his *Theological Essays* caused a storm, and he was dismissed from the Chair of Theology at King's College, London (though in 1866 he was appointed Professor of Moral Philosophy at Cambridge). Tennyson's lyric inviting Maurice to take refuge in his home and garden on the Isle of Wight, written in January 1854, was well known at the time, and is a sincere and modest expression of loyal friendship, solidarity and hospitality.

> Come, when no graver cares employ,
> God-father, come and see your boy:
>   Your presence will be sun in winter,
> Making the little one leap for joy.
>
> For, being of that honest few,
> Who gave the Fiend himself his due,
>   Should eighty-thousand college-councils
> Thunder 'Anathema,' friend, at you;
>
> Should all our churchmen foam in spite
> At you, so careful of the right,
>   Yet one lay-hearth would give you welcome
> (Take it and come) to the Isle of Wight;

38

Where, far from noise and smoke of town,
I watch the twilight falling brown
 All round a careless order'd garden
Close to the ridge of a noble down.

You'll have no scandal while you dine,
But honest talk and wholesome wine,
 And only hear the magpie gossip
Garrulous under a roof of pine:

For groves of pine on either hand,
To break the blast of winter, stand;
 And further on, the hoary Channel
Tumbles a breaker on chalk and sand;

Where, if below the chalky steep
Some ship of battle slowly creep,
 And on thro' zones of light and shadow
Glimmer away to the lonely deep,

We might discuss the Northern sin
Which made a selfish war begin;
 Dispute the claims, arrange the chances;
Emperor, Ottoman, which shall win:

Or whether war's avenging rod
Shall lash all Europe into blood;
 Till you should turn to dearer matters,
Dear to the man that is dear to God;

How best to help the slender store,
How mend the dwellings, of the poor;
 How gain in life, as life advances,
Valour and charity more and more.

Come, Maurice, come: the lawn as yet
Is hoar with rime, or spongy-wet;

But when the wreath of March has blossom'd
Crocus, anemone, violet,

Or later, pay one visit here,
For those are few we hold so dear;
    Nor pay but one, but come for many,
Many and many a happy year.

the Northern sin . . . a selfish war – the Crimean War began in 1853.

9 April

DIETRICH BONHOEFFER

LUTHERAN PASTOR, TEACHER, THEOLOGIAN, POET AND MARTYR, 1945

◄◦►

Powers of Good

Dietrich Bonhoeffer, German, 1906–45, translated by
Reginald Fuller

This New Year's hymn, from Bonhoeffer's *Letters and Papers from Prison*, is a profound expression of the faith and hope in God, and of the deep capacity for love, which Bonhoeffer's life and death exemplify.

With every power for good to stay and guide me,
Comforted and inspired beyond all fear,
I'll live these days with you in thought beside me,
And pass, with you, into the coming year.

The old year still torments our hearts, unhastening;
The long days of our sorrow still endure;
Father, grant to souls thou hast been chastening
That thou hast promised, the healing and the cure.

Should it be ours to drain the cup of grieving
Even to the dregs of pain, at thy command,
We will not falter, thankfully receiving
All that is given by thy loving hand.

But should it be thy will once more to release us
To life's enjoyment and its good sunshine,
That which we've learned from sorrow shall increase us,
And all our life be dedicate as thine.

Today, let candles shed their radiant greeting;
Lo, on our darkness are they not thy light
Leading us, haply, to our longed-for meeting? –
Thou canst illumine even our darkest night.

When now the silence deepens for our hearkening,
Grant we may hear thy children's voices raise
From all the unseen world around us darkening
Their universal paean, in thy praise.

While all the powers of good aid and attend us,
Boldly we'll face the future, come what may.
At even and at morn God will befriend us,
And oh, most surely on each new born day!

10 April

WILLIAM LAW*

PRIEST AND SPIRITUAL WRITER, 1761

————◀◦▶————

From *The Absolute Unlawfulness of the Stage Entertainment, Fully Demonstrated* (1726)

William Law, English, 1686–1761

Law's spiritual classic *A Serious Call to a Devout and Holy Life* (1728) encouraged his readers to live the Christian life to the full, morally and spiritually, and was profoundly influential among English-speaking Christians of the eighteenth and nineteenth centuries. It was a complete and conscientious devotion in all aspects of everyday life that Law was commending in his severe attack on the obscenities of theatre in the earlier work of 1726.

Let it be therefore observed, that the stage is not here condemned, as some other diversions, because they are dangerous, and likely to be occasions of sin; but that it is condemned, as drunkenness and lewdness, as lying and profaneness are to be condemned, not as things that may only be the occasions of sin, but as are in their own nature grossly sinful.

You go to hear a play: I tell you, that you go to hear ribaldry and profaneness; that you entertain your mind with extravagant thoughts, wild rant, blasphemous speeches, wanton amours, profane jests, and impious passions. If you ask me, where is the sin of all this? You may as well ask me, where is the sin of swearing and lying. For it is not only a sin against this or that particular text of Scripture, but it is a sin against the whole nature and spirit of our religion.

43

21 April

ST ANSELM

ARCHBISHOP OF CANTERBURY, AND TEACHER, 1109

———◄◦►———

Laus Deo

Robert Bridges, English, 1844–1930

Anselm's devotional, philosophical and theological writings were profoundly influential in the medieval church, and continue to be so. For 33 years of his adult life Anselm was a monk in the great Benedictine Abbey of Bec, serving as Prior and then Abbot. His intellectual work, his spirituality and ultimately his oversight of the English Church, were rooted in the *Opus Dei*: the regular daily pattern of corporate prayer and praise.

> Let praise devote thy work, and skill employ
> Thy whole mind, and thy heart be lost in joy.
> Well-doing bringeth pride, this constant thought
> Humility, that thy best done is nought.
> Man doeth nothing well, be it great or small,
> Save to praise God; but that hath saved all:
> For God requires no more than thou hast done,
> And takes thy work to bless it for his own.

23 April

ST GEORGE*

MARTYR AND PATRON OF ENGLAND, c.304

———◄◦►———

The Vinegar Cup

Translated from the Arabic of Mu'een Bseiso, Palestinian,
1927–84, by May Jayyusi and Naomi Shihab Nye

Celebrated in the Eastern Church as 'The Great Martyr', and adopted as
Patron of England when his cult was renewed by soldiers returning home
from Palestine after the Crusades, some evidence suggests that George was a
Palestinian Christian, martyred on his native soil at Lydda. Born in Gaza,
Mu'een Bseiso was a literary champion of Palestinian nationalism, for which
he suffered imprisonment and exile. His poem celebrates the life-giving
blood of Jesus spilt into the Palestinian soil – a sacrifice into which the Christian people enter in faith, in eucharistic celebration, and in martyrdom.

> Cast your lots, people,
> Who'll get my robe
> after crucifixion?
>
> The vinegar cup in my right hand,
> the thorn crown on my head,
> and the murderer has walked away free
> while your son has been led
>   to the cross.
> But I shall not run
> from the vinegar cup,
> nor the crown of thorns
> I'll carve the nails of my cross from my own bones
> and continue,
> spilling drops of my blood onto this earth
> For if I should not rip apart
>   how would you be born from my heart?
>   How would I be born from your heart?
>   Oh, my people!

25 April

ST MARK

EVANGELIST

———◄○►———

The Airy Christ (after reading Dr Rieu's translation of St Mark's Gospel)

Stevie Smith, English, 1902–71

Much of Stevie Smith's poetry is an expression of doubt regarding the orthodoxies of Christian faith. On re-reading the Gospel of Mark in Rieu's translation, she is surprised by the freedom and beauty of the 'singer' Christ whose message is not yet bound up in doctrines and moral codes.

Who is this that comes in splendour, coming from the
    blazing East?
This is he we had not thought of, this is he the airy Christ.

Airy, in an airy manner in an airy parkland walking,
Others take him by the hand, lead him, do the talking.

But the Form, the airy One, frowns an airy frown,
What they say he knows must be, but he looks aloofly down,

Looks aloofly at his feet, looks aloofly at his hands,
Knows they must, as prophets say, nailèd be to wooden
    bands.

As he knows the words he sings, that he sings so happily
Must be changed to working laws, yet sings he ceaselessly.

Those who truly hear the voice, the words, the happy song,
Never shall need working laws to keep from doing wrong.

Deaf men will pretend sometimes they hear the song, the
     words,
And make excuse to sin extremely; this will be absurd.

Heed it not. Whatever foolish men may do the song is cried
For those who hear, and the sweet singer does not care that
     he was crucified.

For he does not wish that men should love him more than
     anything
Because he died; he only wishes they would hear him sing.

CHRISTINA ROSSETTI*

POET, 1894

◄◦►

Darkness and light

Christina Rossetti, English, 1830–94

Many of the poems of Rossetti, a devout High Church Anglican, are a candid expression of the struggles of faith and doubt she experienced; illness, a melancholy disposition, and disappointment in personal relationships also caused her much pain. All these find their place within the soul's ongoing relationship with the God who is sometimes hidden, sometimes joyfully disclosed, given here in language of the psalms.

Darkness and light are both alike to Thee:
　Therefore to Thee I lift my darkened face;
Upward I look with eyes that fail to see,
　Athirst for future light and present grace.
　I trust the Hand of Love I scarcely trace.
With breath that fails I cry, Remember me:
　Add breath to breath, so I may run my race
That where Thou art there may Thy servant be.
For Thou art gulf and fountain of my love,
　I unreturning torrent to Thy sea,
　　Yea, Thou the measureless ocean for my rill:
　　Seeking I find, and finding, seek Thee still:
And oh! that I had wings as hath a dove,
Then would I flee away to rest with Thee.

St Catherine of Siena
TEACHER, 1380

——◁◇▷——

Peace of Mind

Kathleen Raine, Scottish, 1908–

Given to contemplative prayer and personal sanctity from an early age, Catherine's wisdom and integrity became widely acknowledged, so that she was involved in many of the fraught political and theological controversies of her native Siena, neighbouring Florence, and even the papacy itself. In the midst of all of these heavy demands upon her, Catherine maintained a profound spirituality which nourished others.

> If the pool were still
> The reflected world
> Of tottering houses,
> The falling cities,
> The quaking mountains
> Would cohere on the surface
>
> And stars invisible
> To the troubled mind
> Be seen in water
> Drawn from the soul's
> Bottomless well.

St Philip and St James
APOSTLES

———◄○►———

What Are Years?

Marianne Moore, American, 1887–1972

Jesus' response to Philip's request that he should satisfy – or convince – the Apostles by showing them the Father is to point him to the mystery of himself and of his relationship with the Father whom he reveals. It is an invitation to contemplation, to a profound acceptance of *what is*, even if that implies uncertainty, suffering or loss. There is something of this same spirit of joyful being and struggling self-acknowledgement in Moore's poem.

> What is our innocence,
> what is our guilt? All are
>   naked, none is safe. And whence
> is courage: the unanswered question,
> the resolute doubt, –
> dumbly calling, deafly listening – that
> in misfortune, even death,
>   encourages others
>   and in its defeat, stirs
>
>   the soul to be strong? He
> sees deep and is glad, who
>   accedes to mortality
> and in his imprisonment rises
> upon himself as
> the sea in a chasm, struggling to be
> free and unable to be,
>   in its surrendering
>   finds its continuing.

So he who strongly feels,
behaves. The very bird,
   grown taller as he sings, steels
his form straight up. Though he is captive,
his mighty singing
says, satisfaction is a lowly
thing, how pure a thing is joy.
    This is mortality,
    this is eternity.

20 May

ALCUIN OF YORK*

DEACON, ABBOT OF TOURS, TEACHER AND POET, 804

————◄◊►————

Whoever stole you from that bush of broom
(Written for his lost nightingale)

Alcuin of York, *c.*740–804, translated from the Latin by
Helen Waddell

A gifted teacher and scholar, among Alcuin's numerous written works is a
Life of St Martin and a celebration of the Church of York composed in
verse, and poems on a wide variety of subjects, one of which is given here.

Whoever stole you from that bush of broom,
　　I think he envied me my happiness,
O little nightingale, for many a time
You lightened my sad heart from its distress,
　　And flooded my whole soul with melody.
And I would have the other birds all come,
　　And sing along with me thy threnody.

So brown and dim that little body was,
　　But none could scorn thy singing. In that throat
That tiny throat, what depth of harmony,
　　And all night long ringing thy changing note.
　　What marvel if the cherubim in heaven
Continually do praise him, when to thee
　　O small and happy, such a grace was given?

21 May

St Helena*

PROTECTRESS OF HOLY PLACES, 330

———◄○►———

From *Helena* (1960)

Evelyn Waugh, English, 1903–66

As an heroic figure – imperial mother of Constantine the Great, builder of significant churches, the renowned pilgrim to the Holy Land who found at Jerusalem pieces of wood from the cross on which Jesus died – Helena was celebrated in one of the earliest English poems, Cynewulf's 'Elene' (eighth century). Waugh's novel opens up the humanity of the saint as she struggles to fulfil her visionary task of finding the sacred relics. Here the pilgrim Empress meditates on the journey of the Magi as the Epiphany liturgy is celebrated in the birthplace of Jesus at Bethlehem (where she founded a great church).

'This is my day,' she thought, 'and these are my kind.'

Perhaps she apprehended that her fame, like theirs, would live in one historic act of devotion; that she too had emerged from a kind of utopia or nameless realm and would vanish like them in the sinking nursery fire-light among the picture-books and the day's toys.

'Like me,' she said to them, 'you were late in coming. The shepherds were here long before; even the cattle. They had joined the chorus of angels before you were on your way. For you the primordial discipline of the heavens was relaxed and a new defiant light blazed amid the disconcerted stars.

'How laboriously you came, taking sights and calculating, where the shepherds had run barefoot! How odd you looked on the road, attended by what outlandish liveries, laden with such preposterous gifts!

'You came at length to the final stage of your pilgrimage and the great star stood still above you. What did you do? You stopped to call on King Herod. Deadly exchange of compliments in which began that unended war of mobs and magistrates against the innocent!

'Yet you came and were not turned away. You too found room before the manger. Your gifts were not needed, but were accepted and put carefully by, for they were brought with love. In that new order of charity that had just come to life, there was room for you, too. You were not lower in the eyes of the holy family than the ox or the ass.

'You are my especial patrons,' said Helena, 'and patrons of all late-comers, of all who have a tedious journey to make to the truth, of all who stand in danger by reason of their talents.

'Dear cousins, pray for me,' said Helena, 'and for my poor overloaded son. May he, too, before the end find kneeling-space in the straw. Pray for the great, lest they perish utterly. And pray for Lactantius and Marcias and the young poets of Trèves and for the souls of my wild, blind ancestors; for their sly foe Odysseus and for the great Longinus.

'For His sake who did not reject your curious gifts, pray always for all the learned, the oblique, the delicate. Let them not be quite forgotten at the Throne of God when the simple come into their kingdom.'

THE VENERABLE BEDE*

SCHOLAR AND POET, 735

———◄◦►———

Bede's Death Song

Old English, from the Letter of St Cuthbert, eighth century,
translated by Mark Pryce

As a biblical scholar and historian, Bede prized language; his writings show
that he regarded poetry as a crucial part of Christian civilization, and as a
gift which is divinely inspired. In his *De Arte Metrica* Bede sets out the craft
and discipline required for the composition of Latin verse, and as his *Ecclesiastical History* contains verse in Old English, we can surmise that he was
steeped in vernacular poetry also (see the entry for St Hilda). This poem,
loosely translated here from Old English, is said to have been repeated by
Bede while he prepared for his death – 'in our own language, as he knew
our poems well', as recorded in a letter written by one of his pupils to
another. It suggests that poetry held for Bede a profound spiritual importance. He is the likely author of the poem.

> No one is wiser than he need be,
> Considering that certain journey which every one must make,
> To take account, before the soul sets out,
> What good there is, and evil,
> With which the spirit may be judged
> After his death day.

THE VISIT OF THE BLESSED VIRGIN MARY TO ELIZABETH

———◄◦►———

True Ways of Knowing

Norman MacCaig, Scottish, 1910–96

This poem unfolds the relationships between objects in the physical world, and celebrates human language as a gift for mutual self-disclosure and self-understanding. In St Luke's Gospel, the wonderful meeting and dialogue between the two cousins Mary and Elizabeth, each pregnant with her first child, is the occasion for revelation and the outpouring of praise. There is a special *way of knowing* between the women, and between mother and child, which involves body, emotions and spirit: an embodied revelation of incarnation which is spoken within the conversation, love and deep trust of friendship.

Not an ounce excessive, not an inch too little,
Our easy reciprocations. You let me know
The way a boat would feel, if it could feel,
The intimate support of water.

The news you bring me has been news forever,
So that I understand what a stone would say
If only a stone could speak. Is it sad a grassblade
Can't know how it is lovely?

Is it sad that you can't know, except by hearsay
(My gossiping failing words) that you are the way
A water is that can clench its palm and crumple
A boat's confiding timbers?

But that's excessive, and too little. Knowing
The way a circle would describe its roundness,
We touch two selves and feel, complete and gentle,
The intimate support of being.

The way that flight would feel a bird flying
(If it could feel) is the way a space that's in
A stone that's in a water would know itself
        If it had our way of knowing.

1 June

ST JUSTIN

MARTYR AT ROME, *c*.165

———◦———

Justin was an early Apologist for the Christian faith, and argued that Christ was the fullness of truth which other philosophies express only partially. His teaching about the Word of God, who has sown the seed of truth in all human beings, finds resonance in the ideas and work of many writers and artists, inspired by the platonic vision that powers of reason and imagination, language and creativity, give expression to the eternal and unchanging beauty and truth of God, which is in all people an 'internal' or spiritual reality. As Wordsworth said, we come into the world 'trailing clouds of glory'; literature, music and art awaken us to our true nature as children of God.

An excerpt from the *Notebooks* of Samuel Taylor Coleridge

Samuel Taylor Coleridge, English, 1774–1834

In looking at objects of Nature while I am thinking, as at yonder moon dim-glimmering through the dewy window-pane, I seem rather to be seeking, as it were *asking* for, a symbolical language for something within me that already and for ever exists, than observing anything new. Even when that latter is the case, yet still I have always an obscure feeling as if that new phenomenon were the dim awaking of a forgotten or hidden truth of my inner nature.

A thought went up my mind to-day

Emily Dickinson, American, 1830–86

A thought went up my mind to-day
That I have had before,
But did not finish, – some way back,
I could not fix the year.

Nor where it went, nor why it came
The second time to me,
Nor definitely what it was,
Have I the art to say.

But somewhere in my soul, I know
I've met the thing before;
It just reminded me — 'twas all —
And came my way no more.

From *The Inner Journey of the Poet*

Kathleen Raine, Scottish, 1908–

. . . since the world of Imagination is the supremely, specifically human universe, the 'kingdom' proper and peculiar to humankind, which we alone inhabit, it is the most real of all worlds. The human world is above all an invisible world of thoughts, feelings and imaginings, experienced not by the body but by the soul. That world does not belong to nature, nor can it be known or measured in natural terms, being of another order, differing from the natural order not in degree but in kind. The inner kingdom has laws of its own, forms of its own, communicated only through the reflected images of painting, music and poetry; which Blake called man's three ways of 'conversing with Paradise'. It is of the very nature of human art to make perceptible the invisible world of the Imagination; for from the very beginnings of human prehistory the forms of art have been not copies of natural appearances (although these have necessarily served as the language of art) but, on the contrary, the expression of that inner order, of the structures, the energies, the living presences within the psyche.

5 June

St Boniface (Wynfrith)

ARCHBISHOP OF MAINZ, MISSIONARY TO GERMANY, AND MARTYR, 754

———◁◇▷———

From *The Song of the Pilgrims*

Rupert Brooke, English, 1887–1915

Wynfrith, as he was originally called, was born and educated in south-west England. His tireless mission among the German peoples, drawing them to Christ, founding monasteries and establishing a stable ecclesiastical structure, has given Boniface the name 'Apostle of Germany'. On one of his many missionary journeys he felled the sacred oak tree of Thor at Geismar, a courageous act which won him many converts. After some time as Archbishop of Mainz, Boniface resigned his see to continue missionary work in Frisia, and was killed by brigands while travelling in 754. Brooke's poem about pilgrimage, written in 1908, is one which reflects on the weary homesickness of journeying and the compelling possibilities of new peoples, cultures and places. Like Boniface, he died while travelling – on a troop ship during World War I, aged 28.

> What light of unremembered skies
> Hast thou relumed within our eyes,
> Thou whom we seek, whom we shall find? . . .
> A certain odour on the wind,
> Thy hidden face beyond the west,
> These things have called us; on a quest
> Older than any road we trod,
> More endless than desire . . .
>   Far God,
> Sigh with thy cruel voice, that fills
> The soul with longing for dim hills
> And faint horizons! For there come
> Grey moments of the antient dumb
> Sickness of travel, when no song

Can cheer us; but the way seems long;
And one remembers . . .
  O Thou,
God of all desirous roaming,
Our hearts are sick of fruitless homing,
And crying after lost desire.
Hearten us onward! As with fire
Consuming dreams of other bliss.
The best Thou givest, giving this
Sufficient thing – to travel still
Over the plain, beyond the hill,
Unhesitating through the shade,
Amid the silence unafraid,
Till, at some sudden turn, one sees
Against the black and muttering trees
Thine altar, wonderfully white,
Among the Forests of the Night.

St Columba

ABBOT OF IONA, AND MISSIONARY, 597

————◀◦▶————

The Holy Isles

Kathleen Raine, Scottish, 1908–

Columba sailed as a missionary from Ireland, settling on the Island of Iona off the west coast of Scotland. There he established a monastery in which Aidan was trained as a monk before he moved southwards to join King Oswald of Northumbria. Aidan made the island of Lindisfarne his base, together with the more remote Farne isles, off the north-east coast of England. Both Lindisfarne and Iona are still places of pilgrimage and renewal, where the divine is encountered in the rhythms of the sea, and in the rising and the setting of the sun. In ancient Celtic culture, the western-most place was regarded as the eternal home to which pilgrim souls tend, and so Iona became an important place for burial.

Lindisfarne

Those whose faces are turned always to the sun's rising
See the living light on its path approaching
As, over the glittering sea where in tide's rising and falling
The sea-beasts bask, on the Isles of Farne
Aidan and Cuthbert saw God's feet walking
Each day towards all who on world's shores await his coming.
There we too, hand in hand, have received the unending
    morning.

Iona

Where, west of the sun, our loved remembered home?
Columba's Eire from Iona's strand
Land-under-wave beyond last dwindling speck
That drops from sight the parting ship
As mourners watch wave after wave break.
Sight follows on its golden wake
A dream returning to its timeless source, the heart
Where all remains that we have loved and known.

11 June

St Barnabas

APOSTLE

———◄◇►———

From *The Muse of History* (1974)

Derek Walcott, St Lucia, West Indies, 1930–

Sharing the title of Apostle with Paul, Barnabas was the man who introduced him to the church (Acts 9), was partner with him in the first
missionary journey, and continued their missionary work in Cyprus once
he and Paul parted (Acts 15). Thus he is one of the great missionaries, and
remembered fondly in Scripture as 'son of consolation' (Acts 4.36) and as
'a good man, full of the Holy Spirit and of faith' (Acts 11.24). In these
words of consolation, Derek Walcott, Nobel Laureate in Literature, argues
that the culture and faith of the 'New World', for both Black and White,
cannot be a lament for the Old, whether African or European. He commends the power of a cultural and religious crucifixion-resurrection: a
carrying forward of tradition into a new vitality which is forged through
bitter experience, conceived in all the violence and disjunction of enslave-
ment, conversion and colonialization, and so *renewed*.

The great poetry of the New World does not pretend to (such)
innocence, its vision is not naïve. Rather, like its fruits, its savour is
a mixture of the acid and the sweet, the apples of its second Eden
have the tartness of experience. In such poetry there is a bitter
memory and it is the bitterness that dries last on the tongue. It is the
acidulous that supplies its energy . . . For us in the archipelago the
tribal memory is salted with the bitter memory of migration.

To such survivors, to all the decimated tribes of the New World
who did not suffer extinction, their degraded arrival must be seen as
the beginning, not the end of our history. The shipwrecks of
Crusoe and of the crew in *The Tempest* are the end of the Old
World . . . To most writers of the archipelago who contemplate
only shipwreck, the New World offers not elation but cynicism, a
despair at the vices of the Old which they feel must be repeated.

Their malaise is an oceanic nostalgia for the older culture and a melancholy at the new, and this can go as deep as a rejection of the untamed landscape, a yearning for ruins. To such writers the death of civilizations is architectural, not spiritual, seeded in their memories is an imagery of vines ascending broken columns, of dead terraces, of Europe as a nourishing museum. They believe in the responsibility of tradition, but what they are in awe of is not tradition, which is alert, alive, simultaneous, but of history, and the same is true of the new magnifiers of Africa. For these their deepest loss is of the old gods, the fear that it is worship which has enslaved progress. Thus the humanism of politics replaces religion. They see such gods as part of the process of history, subjected like the tribe to cycles of process and despair. Because the Old World concept of God is anthropomorphic, the New World slave was forced to make himself in His image, despite such phrases as 'God is light, and in Him is no darkness', and at this point of intersecting faiths the enslaved poet and the enslaved priest surrendered their power. But the tribe in bondage learned to fortify itself by cunning assimilation of the religion of the Old World. What seemed to be surrender was redemption. What seemed the loss of tradition was its renewal. What seemed the death of faith was its rebirth.

RICHARD BAXTER*

HYMN WRITER, 1691

———◆◇◆———

He wants not friends that hath thy love

Richard Baxter, English, 1615–91

Baxter's ministry seems to have borne many of the tensions and animosities of English Christianity during his lifetime. As curate among the weavers of Kidderminster he forged co-operation between the denominations, and though during the Civil War he was an army chaplain with the Parliamentary forces, he disagreed with the more extreme Puritanism of the Commonwealth period. At the Restoration he refused the offer of a bishopric in good conscience, and so was barred from any other ecclesiastical office. He was a man of moderation and a conscientious pastor, but his nonconformity brought him persecution until the last few years of his life. This hymn celebrates the spiritual strength which sustained him during difficult times of isolation: the assurance of God's love for him in Christ, and the fellowship of Christians on earth and in heaven.

> He wants not friends that hath thy love,
> And may converse and walk with thee,
> And with thy Saints here and above,
> With whom for ever I must be.
>
> In the communion of Saints
> Is wisdom, safety and delight;
> And when my heart declines and faints,
> It's raised by their heat and light!
>
> As for my friends, they are not lost;
> The several vessels of thy fleet,
> Though parted now, by tempests tost,
> Shall safely in the haven meet.

Still we are centred all in thee,
Members, though distant, of one Head;
In the same family we be,
By the same faith and spirit led.

Before thy throne we daily meet
As joint-petitioners to thee;
In spirit we each other greet,
And shall again each other see.

The heavenly hosts, world without end,
Shall be my company above;
And thou, my best and surest Friend,
Who shall divide me from thy love?

15 June

EVELYN UNDERHILL*

POET AND SPIRITUAL WRITER, 1941

———◦———

Divine Ignorance (A Saint Speaks)

Evelyn Underhill, English, 1875–1941

Through her writing, teaching and ministry of spiritual guidance, Evelyn Underhill did much to reconnect clergy and lay people with the spiritual traditions of Christianity and to foster in them the desire for spiritual renewal which has blossomed in the contemporary Church through retreats, quiet days and spiritual direction. Here she celebrates the sanctity of the apophatic way.

> This is my prayer, that I shall never find
>   The secret of thy Name;
>   Never attain to bind
> The zone of thought about thy formless flame.
>
> Grant me this grace, that I may never hear
>   The one resolving chord
>   Which shall at last make clear
> The deep harmonic mystery of my Lord.
>
> Shield thou my sense, that I may never know
>   All that thy love can be;
>   Let not my probing go
> To the dread heart of thy divinity.
>
> Wrapped in thy quiet, I do but ask to taste
>   The sweetness of that night;
>   Lost in thy trackless waste,
> There shall the soul find fulhead of delight.
>
> The anguish of thy sacred dark caress,
>   Thy love beyond our span,
>   Self's loss in thine excess:
> These be the torment and the joy of man.

St Alban*

FIRST MARTYR OF ENGLAND, c.250

———◄○►———

Peace

Henry Vaughan, Anglo-Welsh, 1621–95

As a poet Vaughan was conscious of territorial identity: born in mid-Wales, he termed himself 'Silurist', after the ancient British tribe of that area whose name is given by the historian Tacitus as 'Silures'. This poem speaks of a heavenly country formed in the likeness of the incarnate Saviour – one to which Britain's first martyr Alban gave prior allegiance. Bede's *History* says that when Alban was confronted by the military power and force of the Roman authorities in the garrison city of Verulamium (now St Albans), he was 'armed with the Spirit', and refused to renounce his faith. The governor ordered him to be tortured, and then beheaded.

> My Soul, there is a Countrie
>   Far beyond the stars,
> Where stands a winged Centrie
>   All skilfull in the wars;
> There above noise and danger,
>   Sweet peace sits crown'd with smiles,
> And one born in a Manger
>   Commands the Beauteous files.
> He is thy gracious friend,
>   And (O my Soul awake!)
> Did in pure love descend
>   To die here for thy sake.
> If thou canst get but thither,
>   There growes the flower of peace,
> The Rose that cannot wither,
>   Thy fortresse, and thy ease.
> Leave then thy foolish ranges;
>   For none can thee secure,
> But one, who never changes,
>   Thy God, thy life, thy Cure.

THE BIRTH OF ST JOHN THE BAPTIST

———◄◦►———

Hymn for the Nativity of St John Baptist

John Dryden, English, 1631–1700
(First printed as Dryden's by Scott in a Roman Catholic
Primer of hymns, 1706)

These verses tell the wonderful story of John the Baptist's birth from the
first chapter of St Luke's Gospel. In celebrating the birth of the one who is
to announce the Saviour, the poem is a pouring forth of proclamation: the
hills and river speak; the faithful sing; the angel foretells; the doubting,
dumbstruck Zechariah finds voice; the child in the womb acknowledges
his Lord; and the pregnant cousins give thanks, telling one another the
good news of what God is accomplishing in and through them.

> O sylvan prophet! Whose eternal Fame
> Echoes from *Judah's* Hills and *Jordan's* Stream,
> The Musick of our Numbers raise,
> And tune our Voices to thy Praise.
>
> A Messenger from high *Olympus* came
> To bear the Tidings of thy Life and Name,
> And told thy Sire each Prodigy
> That Heav'n design'd to work in thee.
>
> Hearing the News, and doubting in Surprise,
> His faltering Speech in fetter'd Accent dy's;
> But Providence, with happy Choice,
> In thee restor'd thy Father's Voice.
>
> In the Recess of Nature's dark Abode,
> Though still enclos'd, yet knewest thou thy God;
> Whilst each glad parent told and blest
> The Secrets of each other's Breast.

25 June

PRESENTATION OF THE AUGSBURG CONFESSION, 1530/ PHILIPP MELANCHTHON

RENEWER OF THE CHURCH AND SCHOLAR, 1560

————◦————

From *O may I join the choir invisible*

George Eliot (Mary Ann Evans), English, 1819–90

The Confession presented to Emperor Charles V in June 1530, in which the Reformers set out the essential Christian doctrines and asserted basic tenets for the renewal of the Church, was largely the work of Philipp Melanchthon, Luther's friend and foremost intellectual of the German Reformation. In a revised form it remains the key statement of Lutheranism and a foundation document for all Reformed churches. Through the Confession and other works, such as his *Loci Communes* (1521) – a document Elizabeth I revered – and his establishment of the German system of public education, Melanchthon's scholarship and administrative abilities have continued to flourish through the generations in a wealth of intellectual and religious expression. Here the novelist George Eliot, who translated from the German Strauss's *Life of Jesus* (1846) and Feuerbach's *Essence of Christianity* (1854), celebrates those exceptional human beings like Melanchthon who profoundly influence their successors in bequeathing a good example and an enduring foundation upon which others may build.

> O may I join the choir invisible
> Of those immortal dead who live again
> In minds made better by their presence: live
> In pulses stirred to generosity,
> In deeds of daring rectitude, in scorn
> For miserable aims that end with self,
> In thoughts sublime that pierce the night like stars,
> And with their mild persistence urge man's search
> To vaster issues . . .

71

This is the life to come,
Which martyred men have made more glorious
For us who strive to follow. May I reach
That purest heaven, be to other souls
The cup of strength in some great agony,
Enkindle generous ardour, feed pure love,
Beget the smiles that have no cruelty –
Be the sweet presence of a good diffused,
And in diffusion ever more intense.
So shall I join the choir invisible
Whose music is the gladness of the world.

29 June

St Peter and St Paul

APOSTLES

———◀○▶———

Anita Mason's imaginative reconstruction of St Peter's miraculous escape from captivity (Acts 12.6ff.) introduces a sense of fear as his release opens up possibilities of challenge and uncertainty for him which prison seemed to foreclose. Peter is set free to witness to the risen Christ, ultimately (according to ancient tradition) by his death at Rome. Herrick's charming verse celebrates the outstanding witness of St Paul, also believed to have been martyred at Rome, who as 'the least of all the apostles . . . not worthy to be called an apostle' (1 Corinthians 15.9), the convert who continually preached God's grace in Christ, and who in the end 'suffered the loss of all things . . . in order to gain Christ and be found in him' (Philippians 3.7ff.).

From *The Illusionist*, Part IV

Anita Mason, English, 1942–

The chains swung back against the wall and struck it with a clatter that sent his heart pounding. The noise fell away into silence.

The door was open.

He took a step forward and was suddenly afraid. It was safe in the cell. He did not have to do anything. He did not have to make decisions. As long as he was in the cell he did not have to be anywhere else.

He took another step forward. He could not see.

As long as he was in the cell he was asked no questions that he could not answer. As long as he was in the cell he could not make mistakes. As long as he was in the cell he could fail nobody but himself.

He forced himself forward.

As long as he was in the cell he was not asked who he was, because everybody knew who he was. In this place they called him by his real name.

73

'Lord', he whispered.

In front of him, cut out of the blackness, was a rectangle of less impenetrable blackness.

He walked towards it.

He was in the passageway. He turned right, then paused, listening for sounds. He could hear nothing but his own heart. There was a faint greyish light, enough for him to distinguish the walls. It must be early dawn. He began to walk along the passage. He realised he had forgotten his sandals . . .

It was like a dream.

He walked on, through his dream, and came to a flight of steps. He went up it, keeping to the wall, and found himself facing a large door. There was a line of grey light at the bottom of the door, and a cold fresh draught blew on his toes.

His heart was pounding, and his hands shook as he felt for the bolts. They were already drawn back. Resting his weight against the door so that the iron would not scrape, he lifted the latch, then stepped back. The door swung free. He stepped outside.

Beginnings and Endings

Robert Herrick, English, 1591–1674

> *Paul*, he began ill, but he ended well;
> *Judas* began well, but he fouley fell:
> In godlinesse, not the beginnings, so
> Much as the ends are to be lookt unto.

CATHERINE WINKWORTH

HYMN WRITER, 1878

———◄o►———

Deck thyself, my soul, with gladness

Translated from the German of Johannes Franck, 1618–77,
by Catherine Winkworth, English, 1827–78

It was through her interest in the education and role of women in the German churches that Catherine Winkworth first came into contact with the wonderful hymnody of the German Lutheran tradition. Her superb English translations of these hymns in the *Lyra Germanica* of 1853 and 1855, and the *Chorale Book for England* of 1863, were immediately popular in the English-speaking churches, and have enriched worship ever since. These verses express profound wonder and devotion as they consider the mystery of the Eucharist.

> Deck thyself, my soul, with gladness,
> Leave the gloomy haunts of sadness,
> Come into the daylight's splendour,
> There with joy thy praises render
> Unto him whose grace unbounded
> Hath this wondrous banquet founded;
> High o'er all the heavens he reigneth,
> Yet to dwell with thee he deigneth.
>
> Now I sink before thee lowly,
> Filled with joy most deep and holy,
> As with trembling awe and wonder
> On thy mighty works I ponder;
> How, by mystery surrounded,
> Depths no man hath ever sounded,
> None may dare to pierce unbidden
> Secrets that with thee are hidden.

Sun, who all my life dost brighten;
Light, who dost my soul enlighten;
Joy, the sweetest man e'er knoweth;
Fount, whence all my being floweth.
At thy feet I cry, my Maker,
Let me be a fit partaker
Of this blessed food from heaven,
For our good, thy glory, given.

Jesus, Bread of Life, I pray thee,
Let me gladly here obey thee;
Never to my hurt invited,
Be thy love with love requited:
From this banquet let me measure,
Lord, how vast and deep its treasure;
Through the gifts thou here dost give me,
As thy guest in heaven receive me.

ST THOMAS

APOSTLE

————◄◦►————

Up-hill

Christina Rossetti, English, 1830–94

In Chapter 14 of St John's Gospel it is Thomas who interrupts Jesus to ask how the disciples can 'know the way', and who later doubts the resurrection until he has seen and touched the Lord. This poem is a dialogue between an anxious pilgrim soul and the reassuring voice of one who knows the way.

> Does the road wind up-hill all the way?
>   Yes, to the very end.
> Will the day's journey take the whole long day?
>   From morn to night, my friend.

> But is there for the night a resting place?
>   A roof for when the slow dark hours begin.
> May not the darkness hide it from my face?
>   You cannot miss that inn.

> Shall I meet other wayfarers at night?
>   Those who have gone before.
> Then must I knock, or call when just in sight?
>   They will not keep you standing at that door.

> Shall I find comfort, travel-sore and weak?
>   Of labour you shall find the sum.
> Will there be beds for me and all who seek?
>   Yea, beds for all who come.

6 July

THOMAS MORE*

SCHOLAR AND MARTYR, 1535

———◄◦►———

Eye-flattering fortune

Sir Thomas More, English, 1477–1535

More was a brilliant lawyer and thinker, a humanist scholar who counted Erasmus among his friends, a talented raconteur, poet and translator. In his essay *Utopia* (1516) – literally 'Nowhere' – he speculated on the perfect human society of the future while satirizing contemporary trends, and he wrote or assisted in the writing of numerous works refuting Lutheranism and other reforms. His *Dialogue* (1528) was an attack on Tyndale's translation of the Scriptures into the vernacular. While imprisoned in the Tower of London on a charge of high treason for his loyalty to the authority of the Pope, he wrote devotional works and spent his time in penance and prayer. More is said to have written this poem in charcoal after his enemy Thomas Cromwell had visited him with a cruel tale that the King was well disposed towards him, taunting him with the prospect of release.

> Eye-flattering fortune, look thou never so fair
> Nor never so pleasantly begin to smile
> As though thou wouldst my ruin all repair,
> During my life thou shalt not me beguile.
> Trust shall I God, to enter, in a while,
> His haven of heaven, sure and uniform;
> Ever after thy calm look I for a storm.

JAN HUS

SCHOLAR AND MARTYR, 1415

———◄◦►———

From *A Word About Words*

Vaclav Havel, Czech playwright, 1936– , translated by Paul Wilson

Hus translated Wycliffe's writings into Czech and worked for the reform of the Church. He was burnt at the stake for his radical ideas and writings, and quickly became a hero of Czech national identity. This address was written by the radical playwright Vaclav Havel as the acceptance speech for the award of a Peace Prize at the Frankfurt Book Fair in 1989, and read in Havel's absence because he was not free to travel outside the Eastern Bloc. Soon afterwards he was elected President of the post-Communist Czech Republic.

At the beginning of everything is the word.

It is a miracle to which we owe the fact that we are human. But at the same time it is a pitfall and a test, a snare and a trial.

More so, perhaps, than it appears to you who have enormous freedom of speech, and might therefore assume that words are not so important.

They are.

They are important everywhere.

The same word can be humble at one moment and arrogant the next. And a humble word can be transformed easily and imperceptibly into an arrogant one, whereas it is a difficult and protracted process to transform an arrogant word into one that is humble . . .

It is not hard to demonstrate that all the main threats confronting the world today, from atomic war and ecological disaster to a catastrophic collapse of society and civilization – by which I mean the widening of a gulf between rich and poor individuals and nations – have hidden within them a single root cause: the imperceptible transformation of what was originally a humble message into an arrogant one.

Arrogantly, man began to believe that, as the pinnacle and lord of creation, he understood nature completely and could do what he liked with it.

Arrogantly, he began to think that as the possessor of reason, he could completely understand his own history and could therefore plan a life of happiness for all, and that this even gave him the right, in the name of an ostensibly better future for all – to which he had found the one and only key – to sweep from his path all those who did not fall for his plan.

Arrogantly, he began to think that since he was capable of splitting the atom, he was now so perfect that there was no longer any danger of nuclear arms rivalry, let alone nuclear war.

In all these cases he was fatally mistaken. That is bad. But in each case he is already beginning to realize his mistake. And that is good.

Having learned from all this, we should all fight together against arrogant words and keep a weather eye out for any insidious germs of arrogance in words that are seemingly humble.

Obviously this is not just a linguistic task. Responsibility for and towards words is a task which is intrinsically ethical.

As such, however, it is situated beyond the horizon of the visible world, in that realm wherein dwells the Word that was in the beginning and is not the word of man.

St Benedict of Nursia

ABBOT OF MONTE CASSINO AND PATRON OF
EUROPE, *c.*550

————◄◊►————

Pax

D. H. Lawrence, English, 1885–1930

Towards the end of his *Rule* Benedict writes that a religious community
should be an economy of love: 'there is a good spirit which frees us from evil
ways and brings us closer to God and eternal life. It is this latter spirit that all
who follow the monastic way of life should strive to cultivate, spurred on by
fervent love . . . the pure love of one another as of one family should be their
ideal. As for God they should have a profound and loving reverence for him.
They should love their abbot or abbess with sincere and loving affection. They
should value nothing whatever above Christ himself and may he bring us
together to eternal life.' Lawrence has a similar vision of domestic harmony.

All that matters is to be at one with the living God
to be a creature in the house of the God of Life.

Like a cat asleep on a chair
at peace, in peace
and at one with the master of the house, with the mistress,
at home, at home in the house of the living,
sleeping on the hearth, and yawning before the fire.

Sleeping on the hearth of the living world
yawning at home before the fire of life
feeling the presence of the living God
like a great reassurance
a deep calm in the heart
a presence
as of the master sitting at the board
in his own and greater being,
in the house of life.

14 July

JOHN KEBLE*

PRIEST, POET AND RENEWER OF THE CHURCH, 1866

———◄◦►———

From *Morning*

John Keble, English, 1792–1866

Keble's first volume of sacred verse *The Christian Year*, published anony-
mously in 1827, had an immense success. Inspired by the nature poetry of
the Romantics such as Wordsworth, and by the teachings of the Church
Fathers, as a guide to devotion and commentary on the Book of Common
Prayer it found widespread use across the whole spectrum of Anglicanism.
Keble was Professor of Poetry at Oxford from 1831 to 1841, and as a
leader of the High Church Tractarian movement, was much sought after
as a teacher and spiritual guide. He was personally unambitious for high
office, and remained a parish priest all his life. His second volume, *Lyra
Innocentium*, published in 1846, won less acclaim, and some found its devotion to the Blessed Virgin Mary excessive. This excerpt from the opening
poem of *The Christian Year* shows how the purpose of Keble's devotional
poetry is to nourish practical, everyday holiness inspired by traditional
piety and a love of nature.

'His compassions fail not. They are new every morning.'
(Lamentations 3.22, 23)

> Hues of the rich unfolding morn,
> That, ere the glorious sun be born,
> By some soft touch invisible
> Around his path are taught to dwell; –
>
> Thou rustling breeze so fresh and gay,
> That dancest forth at opening day,
> And brushing by with joyous wing,
> Wakenest each little leaf to sing; –

Ye fragrant clouds of dewy steam,
By which deep grove and tangled stream
Pay, for soft rains in season given,
Their tribute to the genial heaven; –

Why waste your treasures of delight
Upon our thankless, joyless sight;
Who day by day to sin awake,
Seldom of heaven and you partake?

Oh! timely happy, timely wise,
Hearts that with rising morn arise!
Eyes that the beam celestial view,
Which evermore makes all things new!

New every morning is the love
Our wakening and uprising prove,
Through sleep and darkness safely brought,
Restored to life, and power, and thought.

New mercies, each returning day,
Hover around us while we pray;
New perils past, new sins forgiven,
New thoughts of God, new hopes of Heaven.

If on our daily course our mind
Be set to hallow all we find,
New treasures still, of countless price,
God will provide for sacrifice.

*   *   *

O could we learn that sacrifice,
What lights would all around us rise!
How would our hearts with wisdom talk
Along Life's dullest dreariest walk!

We need not bid, for cloister'd cell,
Our neighbour and our work farewell,
Nor strive to wind ourselves too high
For sinful man beneath the sky:

The trivial round, the common task,
Would furnish all we need to ask;
Room to deny ourselves; a road
To bring us daily, nearer God.

Seek we no more; content with these,
Let present Rapture, Comfort, Ease,
As Heaven shall bid them, come and go: –
The secret of this Rest below.

22 July

ST MARY MAGDALENE

———◄o►———

From *Taken Care Of* (1965)

Edith Sitwell, English, 1887–1964

In her rather caustic autobiography, written just prior to her death, Dame Edith recalls the good works of her paternal grandmother and the Low Church clergy whom she patronized in 'rescuing' young women perceived to be in moral danger. A long-held view in the Western Church (but not the East) regarded Mary Magdalene as the typical 'fallen woman' who was saved through penitence and reformation. In this tradition, Mary Magdalene, whom Jesus healed of seven devils (Luke 8.2), and who was present at the cross (Mark 15.40), who discovered the empty tomb (Mark 16.1ff.), and to whom the risen Christ appeared (Matthew 28.9; John 20.11ff.), is confused with the notoriously sinful woman who anointed Jesus' feet in the house of Simon (Luke 7.37). Thus misunderstood, in an attitude of self-righteousness rather than sincere love, the saint does not inspire holiness or admiration, but the condescending efforts which Dame Edith mocks here.

My grandmother Sitwell's favourite virtue was, perhaps, that known as charity. But hers was of a peculiar kind.

She had never *really* succeeded in *liking* St Mary Magdalene, who had, to be frank, a rather horrid Roman Catholic air about her. And yet she felt bound to accept her, in a cold manner, owing to the passages in the New Testament. It was, perhaps, owing to this forced acceptance on my grandmother's part that she was determined to wrap equally deplorable persons in an inescapable charity.

Therefore she and a Suffragan Bishop, with his frost-bitten appearance like something on a cheap Christmas card, would, on hot summer evenings at Scarborough, make sorties together in her barouche, driven by her old coachman, Hill. Encircling the town, they would surround and capture any young woman who appeared to them to be unsuitably dressed and in a deplorable 'state of joyosity', as John Knox called it.

85

Aided by Hill, my grandmother and the Bishop would seize these unfortunates and decant them into a red brick house known as The Home, where, supervised by Sister Edith, the matron, a bursting woman like an advertisement for tomatoes in a railway station, they earned their living by tearing our laundry to shreds every week.

It was one of the rules of The Home that every kidnapped young person must, immediately on her arrival, be given a bath under the supervision of Sister Edith. They were then encased in twill night-gowns, like straight waistcoats. Next morning they were forced to put on the Home uniform, hideous navy-blue coats and skirts, and boots worn like policemen in years past. With this attire they wore shapeless navy-blue felt hats. Sister Edith seemed to be bursting out of a parody of a nun's habit; she ascribed this phenomenon to the fact that she was a Deaconess (whatever that may be).

Four times a year the captives were commanded to 'enjoy them-selves'. This entailed bursting into song, accompanied on the harmonium by Sister Edith. The performance started with a solemn rendering of 'The Lost Chord', followed by a singularly horrible setting of John Greenleaf Whittier's 'The Barefoot Boy'. . .

My grandmother and my Aunt Florence entered thoroughly into the 'joyosity'. And the regiment of curates were hoarded like a treasure at the end of the room, and sternly forbidden to look at the captives.

St Bridget (Birgitta) of Sweden
ABBESS OF VADSTENA, AND MYSTIC, 1373

————◄◦►————

From *The Prayers of St Bridget of Sweden*

Bridget was born and married within the Swedish nobility, became the mother of eight children, and led a life of piety and care for others. Upon the death of her husband, Bridget entered the religious life, founding an abbey at Vadstena, of which her daughter, St Catherine, became Abbess. Bridget left Sweden to work for the establishment of her Order of the Most Holy Saviour (called the Bridgettines), and spent the rest of her life based in Rome, making pilgrimages and giving counsel. The greatest Bridgettine convent in England, at Syon House, was one of the first religious institutions to make use of the printing press in its work and mission. Bridget was much revered as a visionary and mystic, and the prayers of the Passion attributed to her have a distinctive beauty.

O Jesus! Inexhaustible Fountain of compassion,
Who in a profound gesture of love
Cried from the Cross 'I thirst!',
Suffering there the thirst for the salvation of the human race.
I beg of Thee, my Saviour,
Inflame within our hearts a yearning towards perfection in all we do,
And extinguish in us the fire of concupiscence
And the passion of earthly desires. Amen.

O Jesus! Strong Lion, Immortal and Invincible King,
Remember the pain which Thou didst endure
When all the strength of Thy body and mind was utterly spent,
Thou didst bow Thy Head and say
'It is finished!'
Through this anguish and grief, I beg of Thee, Lord Jesus,
Have mercy on me in the hour of my death,
When my mind will be in turmoil
And my soul in anguish. Amen.

25 July

St James

APOSTLE

———◄◦►———

Injustice and Praise

Vernon Watkins, Welsh, 1906–67

James was the first of the Apostles to suffer martyrdom; according to Acts 12.2 he was beheaded by Herod Agrippa I in a persecution which also led to Peter's imprisonment. In this poem Vernon Watkins meditates on the integrity and ultimate victory of martyrdom and suffering in the cause of right (echoing some of the theology of 1 Peter).

> When the unjust, uncivil
> Or brutal act wrongs
> A man, and he can call
> No judge to answer the throng's
> Bestial hatred, then
> Not to retaliate
> Against wicked men
> Becomes him and his fate.
>
> If in the ritual
> Of vengeance he live,
> He makes perpetual
> His failure to forgive.
> No; to those arbiters
> Of true behaviour
> There is no strength but stirs
> To honour its saviour.
>
> A tyrant's victory
> Even in the old tales
> Left with the dead the glory

Dropped from unequal scales.
When power on every side
Spelt ruin, defeat,
Never was theme for pride
More certain, more sweet.

Plagues, with hostile weather
Driving from chance or hate
When evils come together
In Job could consecrate
A strictness, a trust
Inviolable. To sing
When taunted by the unjust
Is a most sacred thing.

But what if pride of race
That enemy prove,
How shall a man efface
The inhuman scar on love?
How suffer, not pay back
With sworn antipathy
That scar's degrading lack
Where divine love should be?

Though worst injustice came,
He would be right
Not to sully the name
Which gave him light,
Scourged Christ, by whom the devil
Finds himself outwitted,
Whose breast encounters evil
But cannot commit it.

26 July

ANNE AND JOACHIM*

PARENTS OF THE BLESSED VIRGIN MARY

---◁◦▷---

Joachim and Anne read Proverbs

Mark Pryce, Anglo-Welsh, 1960–

This poem imagines the parents of the Blessed Virgin Mary looking back on the pregnancy of their daughter, contemplating its outrageousness and its mystery. The reference to Proverbs is to Chapter 31, where the virtues of a good wife are extolled.

It was not what we had come to expect of her –
Not after the years of tuition,
Household economics and steady religion,
The careful selection of a decent husband;
Not after all our efforts to ensure
That she should be wise and well provided for
From her own resourcefulness,
An excellent woman –

That sudden (hidden) stain of her child
Before time,
The fearful seeping out of shame,
The tearing of code and convention,
Unravelling us

She surprised:
To her the boy came
Like an unfolding of exquisite cloth for a wedding,
Stuff more precious than ever we could have bought,
More intricate than we could have made with all our care,
She had woven within her,
and (Thank God!) the husband proved better

Than even we had calculated:
He seemed to see her clothed in that same dress,
a garment utterly beyond us,
Gracious, compelling, powerfully modest –
As if our daughter had gained access
To some heavenly loom.

Johann Sebastian Bach, 1750;
Heinrich Schütz, 1672;
George Frederick Handel, 1759

MUSICIANS

———◆———

At a Solemn Musick

John Milton, English, 1608–74

For Milton, choral music has a particular sacredness. It brings to earth the song of the whole company of heaven, and recreates the unity of praise which once joined human beings with the angels and saints before it was fractured at the Fall, and now anticipates the future harmonies of heaven in which humans are called to participate eternally in God's good time.

> Blest pair of sirens, pledges of heaven's joy,
> Sphere-born harmonious sisters, Voice and Verse,
> Wed your divine sounds, and mixed power employ,
> Dead things with inbreathed sense able to pierce,
> And to our high-raised fantasy present
> That undisturbed song of pure concent,
> Aye sung before the sapphire-coloured throne
> To him that sits thereon,
> With saintly shout and solemn jubilee;
> Where the bright seraphim in burning row
> Their loud uplifted angel-trumpets blow,
> And the cherubic host in thousand choirs
> Touch their immortal harps of golden wires,
> With those just spirits that wear victorious palms,
> Hymns devout and holy psalms
> Sing everlastingly;
> That we on earth, with undiscording voice,
> May rightly answer that melodious noise;

As once we did, till disproportioned sin
Jarred against nature's chime, and with harsh din
Broke the fair music that all creatures made
To their great Lord, whose love their motion swayed
In perfect diapason, whilst they stood
In first obedience, and their state of good.
O may we soon renew again that song,
And keep in tune with heaven, till God ere long
To his celestial consort us unite,
To live with him, and sing in endless morn of light.

concent – harmony; *diapason* – harmony.

29 July

Mary, Martha and Lazarus of Bethany

COMPANIONS OF OUR LORD

————◄◦►————

A View of Lazarus

Elizabeth Jennings, English, 1926–2001

As Jesus eats with his friends, sisters Mary and Martha, in the home of their brother Lazarus, whom he has raised from the dead, Mary anoints him with the precious perfume she has bought for his burial (John 12.1–8). Thus Mary proclaims him as the sacrificial victim who is to suffer and die. This poem imagines the earlier scene as Lazarus emerges from the tomb (John 11.38–44). Lazarus is overcome with anguish as the reality to which he returns begins to dawn on him. Is this grief Lazarus expresses at the end of the poem? Does he, like his sister, come to understand that Jesus must take his place in the tomb?

> See he is coming from the tomb. His eyes
> Need shelter from the light. We crowd and press
> Towards him, some say nothing. One or two
> Whisper. Others look afraid but stare,
> Most turn their eyes away. Such a strange
> Light is coming from behind the man
> Brought back from death and coughing in the breeze.
> One by one his senses set to work
> To ease this man to us. A look of loss
> Shows on his features but he does not speak.
> Some begin to question him about
> What dying felt like and how did he break
> Back to us. He can relieve our doubt,
> But he seems dumb and we don't want to make
> His rising difficult although we long
> To look back at the glimmering Kingdom he

94

Has left, if Paradise is there
But is not for the snatching. Lazarus now
Opens his eyes and it's at us he stares
As if we all were strangers. Then it's odd,
But we feel we should stop talking. Lazarus is,
Yes no doubt of it, now shedding tears,
And whispering quietly, God, O no, dear God.

JOHN MASON NEALE
PRIEST AND HYMN WRITER, 1866

———◁◦▷———

O what their joy and their glory must be

Translated from the Latin of Peter Abelard, 1079–1142, by
John Mason Neale, 1818–66

Though he never held high office within the Church of England, John
Mason Neale had a profound and enduring effect upon its worship and
devotional life through his pastoral work and writing; and for English-
speaking Christians in many traditions he has broadened and deepened
Christian prayer and understanding through the hymns he composed, and
especially those he translated from Greek and Latin. Both of the first com-
prehensive English collections of hymns, *Hymns, Ancient and Modern* and
The English Hymnal, contain much of his work, as does *The Lutheran Book
of Worship.* In these verses the medieval theologian Peter Abelard meditates
on the eternal Sabbath which the saints enjoy.

O what their joy and their glory must be,
Those endless Sabbaths the blessed ones see!
Crown for the valiant; to weary ones rest;
God shall be all, and in all ever blest.

What are the Monarch, his court, and his throne?
What are the peace and the joy that they own?
Tell us, ye blest ones, that in it have share,
If what ye feel ye can fully declare.

Truly Jerusalem name we that shore,
'Vision of peace', that brings joy evermore!
Wish and fulfilment can severed be ne'er,
Nor the thing prayed for come short of the prayer.

We, where no trouble distraction can bring,
Safely the anthems of Sion shall sing;
While for thy grace, Lord, their voices of praise
Thy blessed people shall evermore raise.

There dawns no Sabbath, no Sabbath is o'er,
Those Sabbath-keepers have one and no more;
One and unending is that triumph-song
Which to the Angels and us shall belong.

Now in the meanwhile, with hearts raised on high,
We for that country must yearn and must sigh,
Seeking Jerusalem, dear native land,
Through our long exile on Babylon's strand.

Lo before him with our praises we fall,
Of whom, and in whom, and through whom are all;
Of whom, the Father; and through whom, the Son;
In whom, the Spirit, with these ever One.

St Laurence

DEACON AT ROME, AND MARTYR, 258

―――◦――

From *Barchester Towers* (1857), Volume I, Chapter 13

Anthony Trollope, English, 1815–82

The kind and gentle pastor Mr Harding had expected to spend his last years in ministry as the Warden of Hiram's Hospital, a role which he had fulfilled faithfully for many years with solid dependability, according to well-established patterns, but which he had surrendered in humble acquiescence to public calls for 'reform'. After a humiliating interview with the inexperienced and crass bishop's chaplain, Mr Slope, Harding is full of uncertainty as to his capacity to function adequately in a new era where the likes of Slope set the agenda for ministry, and simple goodness no longer seems sufficient. The narrator challenges the tyranny of innovation which characterizes the age: relentless unreflective and unappreciative restructuring, de-stabilizing both Church and society. In a moment of profound self-doubt, Harding wonders whether the painful demands which threaten him are more than he can bear: the equivalent to the holy sufferings of the martyrs, such as St Laurence (San Lorenzo), who according to tradition was roasted on a fiery grid for remaining true to his faith.

Mr Harding was not a happy man as he walked down the palace pathway, and stepped out into the close. His preferment and pleasant house were a second time gone from him; but that he could endure. He had been schooled and insulted by a man young enough to be his son; but that he could put up with. He could even draw from the very injuries, which had been inflicted on him, some of that consolation, which we may believe martyrs always receive from the injustice of their own sufferings, and which is generally proportioned in its strength to the extent of cruelty with which martyrs are treated. He had admitted . . . that he wanted the comfort of his old home, and yet he could have returned to his lodgings in the High Street, if not with exaltation, at least with satisfaction, had that been all. But the venom of the chaplain's harangue had worked into his blood, and sapped the life of his sweet contentments.

'New men are carrying out new measures, and are carting away the useless rubbish of past centuries!' What cruel words these had been; and how often are they now used with all the heartless cruelty of a Slope! A man is sufficiently condemned if it can be shown that either in politics or religion he does not belong to some new school established within the last score of years. He may then be regarded as rubbish and expect to be carted away. A man is nothing now unless he has within him a full appreciation of the new era; an era in which it would seem that neither honesty nor truth is very desirable, but in which success is the only touchstone of merit. We must laugh at everything that is established. Let the joke be ever so bad, ever so untrue to the real principles of joking; nevertheless we must laugh – or else beware the cart. We must talk, think, and live up to the spirit of the times, and write up to it too, if that cacoethes be upon us, or else we are naught. New men and new measures, long credit and few scruples, great success or wonderful ruin, such are now the tastes of Englishmen who know how to live. Alas, alas! Under such circumstances Mr Harding could not but feel that he was an Englishman who did not know how to live. This new doctrine of Mr Slope, new at least at Barchester, sadly disturbed his equanimity . . . When he heard himself designated as rubbish by the Slopes of the world, he had no other resource than to make inquiry within his own bosom as to the truth of the designation. Alas, alas! The evidence seemed generally to go against him.

He had professed in the Bishop's parlour that in these coming sources of the sorrow of the age, in these fits of sad regret from which the latter years of few reflecting men can be free, religion would suffice to comfort him. Yes, religion would console him for the loss of any worldly good; but was his religion of that active sort which would enable him so to repent of misspent years as to pass those that were left to him in a spirit of hope for the future? And such repentance itself, is it not a work of agony and of tears? It is very easy to talk of repentance; but a man has to walk over hot ploughshares before he can complete it; to be skinned alive as was St Bartholomew; to be struck full of arrows as was St Sebastian; to lie broiling on a gridiron like St Lorenzo! How if his past life required such repentance as this? Had he the energy to go through with it?

11 August

ST CLARE OF ASSISI

FOUNDER OF THE MINORESSES
(POOR CLARES), 1253

———◄○►———

From the *First Letter to Blessed Agnes of Prague*

Late thirteenth century, translated by Regis J. Armstrong
and Ignatius C. Brady

These ecstatic verses commending the joy of religious life are taken from
the first of four letters still existing which St Clare wrote to Agnes of
Prague, a Princess of Bohemia. Drawing on liturgical imagery for the feast
of Agnes' namesake, the 13-year-old virgin-martyr St Agnes (304), St
Clare praises Christ the Bridegroom whom the soul weds in the spiritual
intimacy of chastity, poverty and obedience. Agnes, like Clare, set aside a
life of wealthy privilege and the dynastic obligations of marriage for the
freedom and simplicity of religious community, in the spirit of St Francis.

When You have loved, You shall be chaste;
When You have touched, You shall become pure;
When You have accepted, You shall be a virgin.
Whose power is stronger,
Whose generosity is more abundant,
Whose appearance more beautiful,
Whose love more tender,
Whose courtesy more gracious.
In Whose embrace You are already caught up;
Who has adorned Your breast with precious stones
    And has placed priceless pearls in Your ears
    and has surrounded You with sparkling gems
    as though blossoms of springtime
    and placed on Your head a golden crown
    as a sign to all of Your holiness.

11 August

JOHN HENRY NEWMAN*
PRIEST, TEACHER, NOVELIST AND HYMN WRITER, 1890

———◄◉►———

From *Apologia pro Vita Sua*
John Henry Newman, English, 1801–90

Now regarded as a classic of spiritual autobiography, and a masterpiece of English prose, what was later published as Newman's *Apologia* first appeared serially in 1864, in answer to Charles Kingsley's charge that Newman did not respect truth. As a leader of the Oxford Movement and convert to Roman Catholicism, Newman was one of the most influential and fiercely contested of English-speaking Christians in the nineteenth century. Some of his theology seems to prefigure what his adopted Church came later to recognize in the Second Vatican Council, and his poems and hymns continue to inspire believers across many denominations.

If I looked into a mirror, and did not see my face, I should have the sort of feeling which actually comes upon me, when I look into this living busy world, and see no reflection of its Creator . . . Were it not for this voice, speaking so clearly in my conscience and my heart, I should be an atheist or pantheist, or a polytheist when I looked into the world . . . The sight of the world is nothing else than the prophet's scroll, full of 'lamentations, and mourning and woe'.

To consider the world in its length and breadth, its various history, the many races of man, their starts, their fortunes, their mutual alienation, their conflicts; and then their ways, habits, governments, forms of worship; their enterprises, their aimless courses, their random achievements and acquirements, the impotent conclusion of long standing facts, the tokens so faint and broken of a superintending design, the blind evolution of what turn out to be great powers or truths, the progress of things, as if from unreasoning

101

elements, not towards final causes, the greatness and littleness of man, his far-reaching aims, his short duration, the curtain hung over his futurity, the disappointments of life, the defeat of good, the success of evil, physical pain, mental anguish, the prevalence and intensity of sin, the pervading idolatries, the corruptions, the dreary hopeless irreligion, that condition of the whole race, so fearfully yet exactly described in the Apostle's words, 'having no hope and without God in the world.' . . .

What shall be said to this heart-piercing, reason-bewildering fact? I can only answer, that either there is no Creator, or this living society of men is in a true sense discarded from His presence . . . *If* there be a God, *since* there is a God, the human race is implicated in some terrible aboriginal calamity. It is out of joint with the purposes of its Creator. This is a fact, a fact as true as the fact of its existence; and thus the doctrine of what is theologically called original sin becomes to me almost as certain as that the world exists, and the existence of God.

JEREMY TAYLOR*

BISHOP AND TEACHER, 1667

◄◦►

A cheerful spirit

From a sermon of Bishop Jeremy Taylor, English, 1613–67

Introducing a selection of George Herbert's poems, W. H. Auden wrote that Herbert's poetry and Jeremy Taylor's prose are 'together . . . the finest expression we have of Anglican piety at its best'.

A cheerful spirit is the best convoy for religion; and though sadness does in some cases become a Christian, as being an index of a pious mind, of compassion, and a wise proper resentment of things, yet it serves but one end, being useful in the only instance of repentance; and hath done its greatest works, not when it weeps and sighs, but when it hates and grows careful against sin. But cheerfulness and a festival spirit fills the soul full of harmony, it composes music for Churches and for hearts, it makes and publishes glorifications of God, it produces thankfulness and serves the end of charity, and when the oil of gladness runs over, it makes bright and tall emissions of light and holy fires, reaching up to a cloud, and making joy round about. And therefore since it is so innocent, and may be so pious and full of holy advantage, whatsoever can innocently minister to this holy joy does set forward the work of religion and charity.

And indeed charity itself, which is the vertical top of all religion, is nothing else but an union of joys, concentred in the heart, and reflected from all the angles of our life and intercourse. It is a rejoicing in God, a gladness in our neighbour's good, a pleasure in doing good, a rejoicing with him; and without love we cannot have any joy at all. It is this that makes children to be a pleasure, and friendship to be so noble and divine a thing; and on this account it is certain that all that which can innocently make a man cheerful, does also make him charitable; for grief, and age, and sickness, and weariness, these are peevish and troublesome; but mirth and cheerfulness is content, and civil, and compliant, and communicative, and loves to do good, and swells up to felicity only upon the wings of charity.

In this account is pleasure enough for a Christian, and if a cheerful discourse and an amicable friendly mirth can refresh the spirit, and take it off from the vile temptations of peevish, despairing, uncomplying melancholy, it must needs be innocent and commendable. And we may as well be refreshed by a clean and brisk discourse, as by the air of Campanian wines; and our faces and our heads may as well be anointed and look pleasant with wit and friendly intercourse, as with the fat of the balsam tree; and such a conversation no wise man ever did or ought to reprove. But when the jest hath teeth and nails, biting or scratching our Brother, when it is loose and wanton, when it is unseasonable, and much, or many; when it serves ill purposes, or spends better time, then it is the drunkenness of the soul, and makes the spirit fly away, seeking for a Temple where the mirth and the music is solemn and religious.

15 August

THE BLESSED VIRGIN MARY

——◄◊►——

Her Virgin eyes saw God incarnate born
Thomas Ken, English, 1637–1711

Written by a High Church Anglican in the Laudian tradition, who led his life according to the strictest principles of conscience and asceticism, Bishop Ken's hymn accords to Mary the honour which she is to enjoy through all generations: as Second Eve, she is representative of the human race redeemed in Christ; as mother of the Saviour, first among the saints in heaven.

> Her Virgin eyes saw God incarnate born,
> When she to Bethl'em came that happy morn;
> How high her raptures then began to swell,
> None but her own omniscient Son can tell.
>
> As Eve when she her fontal sin reviewed,
> Wept for herself and all she should include,
> Blest Mary with man's Saviour in embrace
> Joyed for herself and for all human race.
>
> All Saints are by her Son's dear influence blest,
> She kept the very Fountain at her breast;
> The Son adored and nursed by the sweet Maid
> A thousandfold of love for love repaid.
>
> Heaven with transcendent joys her entrance graced,
> Next to his throne her Son his Mother placed;
> And here below, now she's of heaven possest,
> All generations are to call her blest.

20 August

St Bernard of Clairvaux
ABBOT AND TEACHER, 1153

———◄◊►———

From *Clairvaux*

Thomas Merton, American, 1915–68

In this poem Merton explores the beauty of the abbey buildings at Clairvaux, established by Bernard in 1115. He finds that they embody both the
contemplative severity and the mutual love which he seeks in community
life as a member of the Cistercian Order.

'Hidden in this heaven-harbor
Wood-cradle valley, narrow and away from men,
Bernard built me, model of all solitudes,
Picture of contemplation and of love, the figure of all prayer
Clairvaux cloister.'

Abbey, whose back is to the hills whose backs are to the
    world,
Your inward look is ever resting
Upon your central garth and garden, full of sun,
Your catch-light cloister.
In-turning, Peace-finding, living in a mirror that attracts the
    noon
You look at deep all-heaven in the pool: your heart,
Down-looking, not up, within, not out,
Downdrawing all the sky into your quiet
Well or pool or mirror-lake of clear humility.

Holy, immense, the arching air,
The vaulted heaven, full of liberty,
That never even notices the continents,
Passing them forever by, in fleets of light,

Sees you, Clairvaux, and is astounded by the confidence
    Of your expectancy,
Leans down into your loving and wide-open heart
And loves you, who have kept yourself for the blue sky
    alone,
And know no other landscape, and no other view.
O white, O modest cloister,
Shy cloister, Heaven is your prisoner.
He comes to earth and hides His image in your heart
Where He may rest unseen by the grey, grasping,
Jealous, double-dealing world:
The day that flies the complicated alleys
And the blind yards, and covered squares, and wall-eyed
    markets
Fills your clean court with seas of peace.

But oh, how all the light-and-shaded bays are garlanded with
    life,
With brotherlife, slow growing in the fruitful silence,
In this tender sun,
Clinging in strength to these safe walls, and one another,
All interlacing, in the light, as close as vines:
Godlove in all their ways and gestures flowering
And God's peace giving firstfruits in their quietude.

O holy Bernard, wise in brotherlove,
Vintner who train and grow, and prune and tie us
Fast, trim us in sure and perfect arbors of stability and rule:
You have forseen what vintages the Holy Spirit,
Ripening, in our concord, as in vine-vein the strong sun,
Will trample in His press, His charity, in the due day,
To barrel us, His Burgundy.

24 August

ST BARTHOLOMEW

APOSTLE

———◄○►———

He could not be hidden

Jane Sahi, Indian

According to Eusebius, the historian of the early Church, a second-century missionary, St Pantaenus, found in India a copy of the Gospel of Matthew which had been taken there by Bartholomew the Apostle. This poem by an Indian Christian is a meditation on the incident in Matthew 15.21–8, where a gentile woman, a 'foreigner' of Canaanite origin, comes to Jesus in faith, and sees in him the healing power of God which is for all people and all nations.

> He could not be hidden
> In the outhouse of an inn,
> Nor in small-town, down-town Nazareth
> Nor in the bosom of his family.
> He could not escape from the crowd
> To the singing hills, and waters of Galilee.
> His secrets became the rage of the town,
> He could not perform, or conform
> To the wail or the pipings of
> The petulant children of Israel.
> He could not pass unnoticed
> In upmarket holy Jerusalem
> But causes a furore midst
> The cages and tables and changers.
> He would not be nailed down,
> Bouldered in;
> But quietly, for ever, stepped over the rim
> And now our hidden longings
> Are starlit, but secret in Him.

28 August

ST AUGUSTINE OF HIPPO

BISHOP AND TEACHER, 430

————◄◦►————

From *Confessions* IX, vi–vii

Translated by Henry Chadwick, English, 1920–

In this excerpt from the spiritual reflections on his life Augustine recalls his experience of the power of hymns to move and inspire him. The singing of hymns was a practice only in the Eastern Church until they were introduced at Milan by Bishop Ambrose – according to Augustine, as protest songs against the Arian party which he opposed!

During those days I found an insatiable and amazing delight in considering the profundity of your purpose for the salvation of the human race. How I wept during your hymns and songs! I was deeply moved by the music of the sweet chants of your Church. The sound flowed into my ears and the truth was distilled into my heart. This caused the feelings of devotion to overflow. Tears ran, and it was good for me to have that experience.

The church at Milan had begun only a short time before to employ this method of mutual comfort and exhortation. The brothers used to sing together with both heart and voice in a state of high enthusiasm. Only a year or a little more had passed since Justinia, mother of the young king Valentinian, was persecuting your servant Ambrose in the interest of her heresy. She had been led into error by the Arians. The devout congregation kept continual guard in the Church, ready to die with their bishop, your servant. There my mother, your handmaid, was a leader in keeping anxious watch and lived in prayer. We were still cold, untouched by the power of your spirit, but were excited by the tension and disturbed atmosphere in the city. That was the time when the decision was taken to introduce hymns and psalms sung after the custom of the eastern Churches, to prevent the people from succumbing to depression and exhaustion. From that time to this day the practice has been retained and many, indeed almost all your flocks, in other parts of the world have imitated it.

THE BEHEADING OF
ST JOHN THE BAPTIST*

———◄◊►———

Reward

R. S. Thomas, Welsh, 1913–2000

R. S. Thomas takes Herod's reckless promise to the dancing daughter of Herodias (Matthew 14.1ff.) as a metaphor for contemporary culture, in which spiritual values are mortgaged for more immediate gratification: the allure of technological progress comes ultimately to possess not simply our patterns of thought, but the very essence of who we are as human beings.

> 'Dance for me,' time
> says. 'Half of my kingdom
> if you dance well.'
> The machine does so
>
> Coming with its request
> At the end not
> For humanity's head but
> Its heart on a platter.

30 August [LBW 31 August]

JOHN BUNYAN

SPIRITUAL WRITER, 1688

———◄◦►———

From *The Pilgrim's Progress from This World to That Which Is To Come: Delivered Under the Similitude of a Dream*

John Bunyan, English, 1628–88

As the full title of Bunyan's great allegorical work sets out, *The Pilgrim's Progress* is the story of Christian's journey through life towards spiritual maturity and freedom, found ultimately beyond death. In this scene towards the end of the tale, Christian and his companion Hopeful draw within sight of the heavenly city, and face the last challenge of their long pilgrimage. Though he is so close to fulfilment, Christian is almost wholly overcome by the experience of dying, and believes himself lost: no amount of experience and no depth of sanctity can replace the constant need for God's grace.

Now I further saw that betwixt them and the Gate was a River, but there was no Bridge to go over, the River was very deep; at the sight therefore of this River, the pilgrims were much stounded, but the men that went with them said, You must go through, or you cannot come at the Gate.

The Pilgrims then began to enquire if there was no other way to the Gate; to which they answered, Yes, but there hath not any, save two, to wit, Enoch and Elijah, been permitted to tread that path, since the foundation of the World, nor shall, until the last Trumpet shall sound. The Pilgrims then, especially Christian, began to dispond in his mind, and looked this way and that, but no way could be found by them, by which they might escape the River. Then they asked the men if the Waters were all of a depth. They said, No; yet they could not help them in that Case, for said they: You shall find it deeper or shallower, as you believe in the King of the place.

Then they addressed themselves to the Water; and entring, Christian began to sink, and crying out to his good friend Hopeful; he said, I sink in deep Waters, the Billows go over my head, all his Waves go over me.

Then said the other, Be of good chear my Brother, I feel the bottom, and it is good. Then said Christian, Ah my friend, the sorrows of death have compassed me about, I shall not see the Land that flows with Milk and Honey. And with that, a great darkness and horror fell upon Christian, so that he could not see before him; also here he in great measure lost his senses, so that he could neither remember nor orderly talk of any of those sweet refreshments that he had met with in the way of his Pilgrimage. But all the words that he spake, still tended to discover that he had horror of mind, and hearty fears that he should die in that River, and never obtain entrance in at the Gate: here also, as they that stood by perceived, he was much in the troublesome thoughts of the sins that he had committed, both since and before he began to be a Pilgrim. 'Twas also observed, that he was troubled with apparitions of Hobgoblins and Evil Spirits. Forever and anon he would intimate so much by his words. Hopeful therefore had much adoe to keep his Brothers head above water, yea sometimes he would be quite gone down, and then ere a while he would rise up again half dead. Hopeful also would endeavour to comfort him, saying, Brother, I see the Gate, and men standing by it to receive us. But Christian would answer: 'Tis you, 'tis you they wait for, you have been Hopeful ever since I knew you. And so have you, said he to Christian. Ah Brother, said he, surely if I was right, he would now arise to help me; but for my sins he hath brought me into the snare, and hath left me. Then said Hopeful, My Brother, you have quite forgot the Text, where it said of the wicked, *There is no band in their death, but their strength is firm, they are not troubled as other men, neither are they plagued like other men.* These troubles and distresses that you go through in these Waters, are no sign that God hath forsaken you, but are sent to try you, whether you will call to mind that which heretofore you have received of his goodness, and live upon him in your distress.

Then I saw in my Dream, that Christian was in a muse a while; To whom also Hopeful added this word, *Be of good chear, Jesus Christ maketh thee whole*: And with that, Christian brake out with a loud voice, Oh I see him again! And he tells me, *When thou passest through the waters, I will be with thee, and through the Rivers, they shall not overflow thee*. Then they both took courage, and the enemy was after that as still as a stone, until they were gone over. Christian therefore presently found ground to stand upon; and so it followed that the rest of the River was but shallow. Thus they got over.

2 September

NIKOLAI GRUNDTVIG
BISHOP, RENEWER OF THE CHURCH AND HYMN WRITER, 1872

———◄◦►———

Lord, from you we cannot flee
Translated from the Danish by Kenneth Stevenson, English, 1949–

The Lutheran Book of Worship contains several hymns written by Grundtvig. In this hymn, translated as a prose poem, Grundtvig meditates with devotion and pastoral realism on Jesus' words in Chapter 6 of St John's Gospel: 'I am the Bread of Life'.

Lord, from you we cannot flee,
you who are the friend of souls,
the Son of the Living God.
The goal of our faith,
the only being on earth
in whose mouth is the word of life.

Your word cannot frighten us away,
even when it sounds harshly in our ears.
For we feel deep within us
that on earth death is the uniquely harsh word
and that what breathes life into it again
is bled from you as a labour of sheer love.

'Eat my flesh and drink my blood' –
says the good Prince of Life –
' – on my word, with bread and wine.
My death, it was for you.
My resurrection from the dark earth,
it was for you.'

My going ahead of you into heaven,
it was for you.

Listen, my heart, beating within my breast
with anxious thoughts.
Take our Lord at his word, taste him
at his table of grace.
Eat his flesh and drink his blood,
and rise up, as he did, to new life.

The King of heaven's Son speaks
and bears witness:
'Anyone who shares in my flesh and blood,
with a good will has my life in him,
just as my Father's life is in me.'

This is the secret known on earth
to Jesus and his community.
The world considers it vanity,
but the heart feels
that truly down to the very dust itself
has stooped the life that dwells
in the love of God.

3 September

St Gregory the Great
BISHOP OF ROME, AND TEACHER, 604

————◄○►————

A life of hope deferred
From *Time Flies*, Christina Rossetti, English, 1830–94

It was Pope Gregory who sent Augustine and his companions to evange-
lize southern England, and though he was often wracked with acute pain
from illness and beset with many problems in Rome, he continued to give
the missionaries hope and direction when the task seemed overwhelming.
As the mission took root, Gregory came to be revered as the spiritual
father of English Christianity, and some of the earliest Christian poetry is
shot through with the influence of his homilies and other writings. In his
history of the English Church, Bede celebrates Gregory as the Apostle of
the English: 'He sent other missionaries in his place; but it was his prayers
and encouragement that made their mission fruitful' (II.1). Rossetti's
poem suggests something of the character of Gregory's leadership.

> A life of hope deferred too often is
> A life of wasted opportunities;
> A life of perished hope too often is
> A life of all-lost opportunities:
> Yet hope is but the flower and not the root,
> And hope is still the flower and not the fruit; –
> Arise and sow and weed: a day shall come
> When also thou shalt keep thy harvest home.

THE BIRTH OF THE
BLESSED VIRGIN MARY

——◁◦▷——

Grace

Judith Wright, Australian, 1915–2000

This poem celebrates the divinity which floods 'ordinary' life and the
miracle of grace which is everywhere and yet especially apparent in certain
people.

> Living is dailiness, a simple bread
> That's worth the eating. But I have known a wine,
> A drunkenness that can't be spoken or sung
> Without betraying it. Far past Yours or Mine,
> Even past Ours, it has nothing at all to say;
> It slants a sudden laser through the common day.
>
> It seems to have nothing to do with things at all,
> Requires another element or dimension.
> Not contemplation brings it; it merely happens,
> Past expectation and beyond intention;
> Takes over the depth of flesh, the inward eye,
> Is there, then vanishes. Does not live or die,
> Because it occurs beyond the here and now,
> Positives, negatives, what we hope and are.
> Not even being in love, or making love,
> Brings it. It plunges a sword from a dark star.
>
> Maybe there was once a word for it. Call it grace.
> I have seen it, once or twice, through a human face.

HOLY CROSS DAY

———◦———

Vexilla Regis

Venantius Fortunatus, Venetian, *c.*530–610, translated from Latin
by John Mason Neale

As well as hymns, Venantius Fortunatus wrote many books of poetry and metrical lives of the saints. In his work the formality of classical antiquity combines with the devotional symbolism of medieval Europe. This exaltation of the cross is one of his most beautiful compositions.

> The royal banners forward go;
> The Cross shines forth in mystic glow;
> Where he in flesh, our flesh who made,
> Our sentence bore, our ransom paid:
>
> Where deep for us the spear was dyed,
> Life's torrent rushing from his side,
> To wash us in that precious flood,
> Where mingled Water flowed, and Blood.
>
> Fulfilled is all that David told
> In true prophetic song of old;
> Amidst the nations, God, saith he,
> Hath reigned and triumphed from the tree.
>
> O Tree of beauty, Tree of light!
> O Tree with royal purple dight!
> Elect on whose triumphal breast
> Those holy limbs should find their rest:
>
> On whose dear arms, so widely flung,
> The weight of this world's ransom hung:
> The price of humankind to pay,
> And spoil the spoiler of his prey.

18 September

DAG HAMMARSKJÖLD

PEACEMAKER, 1961

———◄◇►———

The moon was caught in the branches

Dag Hammarskjöld, Swedish, 1905–61. From *Markings*,
translated by Leif Sjöberg and W. H. Auden

Remembered as a peacemaker, Hammarskjöld's statement that 'In our age,
the road to holiness necessarily passes through the world of action' was
given full expression in his own life in high office as civil servant, politi-
cian, and finally as Secretary-General of the United Nations. He died in
the course of his duties in 1961. In this poem he reflects upon the loneli-
ness of Jesus in Gethsemane, and the immense love required of him.

> The moon was caught in the branches:
> Bound by its vow,
> My heart was heavy.
>
> Naked against the night
> The trees slept. 'Nevertheless,
> Not as I will . . .'
>
> The burden remained mine:
> They could not hear my call,
> And all was silence.
>
> Soon, now, the torches, the kiss:
> Soon the grey of dawn
> In the Judgement Hall.
>
> What will their love help there?
> There, the question is only
> If I love them.

21 September

ST MATTHEW

APOSTLE AND EVANGELIST

————◄◦►————

September Sun: 1947

David Gascoyne, English, 1916–2002

This poem expresses the terrible uncertainty of the nuclear age, in which
the human race is spiritually blind and materially obsessed, on the brink of
utter destruction. Yet the hope and prayer is for a purging and for a
growth in Gospel values so that 'the righteous may shine like the sun'
(Matthew 13.43).

Magnificent strong sun! in these last days
So prodigally generous of pristine light
That's wasted only by men's sight that will not see
And by self-darkened spirits from whose night
Can rise no longer orison or praise:

Let us consume in fire unfed like yours
And may the quickened gold within me come
To mintage in due season, and not be
Transmuted to no better end than dumb
And self-sufficient usury. These days and years

May bring the sudden call to harvesting,
When if the fields Man labours only yield
Glitter and husks, then with an angrier sun may He
Who first with His gold seed the sightless field
Of Chaos planted, all our trash to cinders bring.

ST MICHAEL AND ALL ANGELS

————◄◦►————

Michael Militant

Translated from the Gaelic by Alexander Carmichael, Scottish,
1832–1912

This is a prayer for angelic company, guidance and protection along life's
journey. Michael's militancy is a watchfulness which guards and defends
the vulnerable pilgrim.

O Michael Militant, thou King of the angels,
Shield thy people with the power of thy sword;
Shield thy people with the power of thy sword.

Spread thy wing over sea and land,
East and west, and shield us from the foe;
East and west, and shield us from the foe.

Brighten thy feast from heaven above,
Be with us in the pilgrimage, in the twistings of the fight;
Be with us in the pilgrimage, in the twistings of the fight

Thou chief of chiefs, thou chief of the needy,
Be with us in the journey, and in the gleam of the river;
Be with us in the journey, and in the gleam of the river.

Thou chief of chiefs, thou chief of angels,
Spread thy wing over sea and land,
For thine is their fullness, thine is their fullness;
Thine own is their fullness, thine own is their fullness.

30 September

ST JEROME

TRANSLATOR AND TEACHER OF THE FAITH, 420

————◀◎▶————

'St Jerome', from *Two Desert Fathers*

Thomas Merton, American, 1915–68

Here Merton reflects on the remarkable personality and achievements of
Jerome, which still speak powerfully and dangerously today: the period he
spent as a hermit in the Syrian desert, and also his time in the great cities of
the Roman Empire, before settling at Bethlehem in 386, founding a
monastery and devoting himself to study. Jerome's scholarship was exceptional, and his capacity for language bore fruit wonderfully in his
translation of most of the Bible into Latin. He was as contentious as he was
ascetical, and his critique could be severe.

> The light that rises on Jehosaphat
> Greyer than the rocks
> On which the Baptist stood and preached,
> Showed you the coming of the solemn Christ.
> You heard his speech proceeding like an army
> Before Whose tread all understanding shall succumb
> Knowing no way of withstanding the weight of
> His language
> Or the keen, bright, two-way sword-measure
> Of that Judgement.

> The light that sank upon the valley of the final settlement
> Showed you over and over the wreckage of the universe
> Boiling like wine out of the faucets of that ruined stadium
> Far bloodier than the vintage of those evenings in the
> trampled west.

> Jerome! Jerome!

What is this voice comes down to us
Down the far tunnels from the heaven of your solitude?
You who have died hard by the caves of Bethlehem
Forgotten by the barren world, the hater of the Incarnation,
Oh, now, how suddenly risen again
You chide us with that language loud with fight:
Language of one who had to wrestle in the long
    Night's wilderness
With the wild angel, Revelation.

Words were not made to dress such lightning
And thought cracks under the pressure of that thunder
When your most learned, mad
And immaculate indignation

Sunders with its meteors the darkness of our classic
    Intellection,
Severs our midnight like a streak of flying Pullmans
And challenges our black unhappiness
Lord as the lights of an express.

DEDICATION OF A CHURCH

IF DATE UNKNOWN

——◄◦►——

From *Churches*

Thomas Traherne, English, 1637–74

Traherne's idiosyncratic spelling has been left unaltered in this portion of his poem celebrating the architectural and artistic beauty of church buildings, which never lapses into an idolatry of physical structures, however ancient or delightful. The building is always associated with the community of Christians who assemble there for the worship of God.

> Those stately Structures which on Earth I view
> To GOD erected, whether Old or New;
> His Sacred Temples which the World adorn,
> Much more than Mines of Ore or Fields of Corn,
> My Soul delight: How do they please mine Ey
> When they are fill'd with Christian Family!
> Upon the face of all the peopled Earth
> There's no such sacred Joy or solemn Mirth,
> To pleas and satisfy my Heart's Desire,
> As that wherewith my Lord is in a Quire,
> In holy Hymns by warbling Voices prais'd,
> With Eys lift up, and joint Affections rais'd.
>
> The Arches built (like Hev'n) wide and high
> Shew his Magnificence and Majesty
> Whose House it is: With so much Art and Cost
> The Pile is fram'd, the curious Knobs embost,
> Set off with Gold, that me it doth more pleas
> Than Princes Courts or Royal Palaces;
> Great Stones pil'd up by costly Labors there
> Like Mountains carv'd by human Skill appear;
> Where Towers, Pillars, Pinnacles, and Spires
> Do all concur to match my great Desires,
> Whose Joy it is to see such Structures rais'd
> To th'end my God and Father should be prais'd.

4 October

ST FRANCIS OF ASSISI

FRIAR AND DEACON, 1226

———◄○►———

From *De Profundis*

Oscar Wilde, Irish, 1854–1900

Written in 1897 when Wilde was in public disgrace, serving a prison sentence and declared bankrupt, this letter arises out of the depths of Wilde's humiliation. In his reflections on human suffering and repentance, Wilde writes eloquently of the graciousness of Christ's 'poetic' nature – that is, of the supreme quality of his imagination – and of his sympathy and love towards others. For Wilde, only the life of St Francis truly mirrored these qualities of Christ.

The world had always loved the saint as being the nearest approach to the perfection of God. Christ, through some divine instinct in him, seems to have always loved the sinner as being the nearest possible approach to the perfection of man. His primary desire was not to reform people, any more than his primary desire was to relieve suffering. To turn an interesting thief into a tedious honest man was not his aim. He would have thought little of the Prisoners' Aid Society and other modern movements of that kind. The conversion of a publican into a Pharisee would not have seemed to him a great achievement. But in a manner not yet understood of the world he regarded sin and suffering as being in themselves beautiful holy things and modes of perfection.

It seems a very dangerous idea. It is – all great ideas are dangerous. That it was Christ's creed admits of no doubt. That it is the true creed I don't doubt myself.

Of course the sinner must repent. But why? Simply because otherwise he would be unable to realize what he had done. The moment of repentance is the moment of initiation. More than that: it is the means by which one alters one's past. The Greeks thought that impossible. They often say in their gnomic aphorisms, 'Even the Gods cannot alter the past'. Christ showed that the commonest sinner could do it, that it was the one thing he could do. Christ, had he been asked, would have said – I feel quite certain about it – that the moment the prodigal son fell on his knees and wept, he made his having wasted his substance with harlots, his swine-herding and hungering for the husks they ate, beautiful and holy moments in his life. It is difficult for most people to grasp the idea. I dare say one has to go to prison to understand it. If so, it may be worth while going to prison.

There is something so unique about Christ. Of course just as there are false dawns before the dawn itself, and winter days so full of sudden sunlight that they will cheat the wise crocus into squandering its gold before its time, and make some foolish bird call to its mate to build on barren boughs, so there were Christians before Christ. For that we should be grateful. The unfortunate thing is that there have been none since. I make one exception, St Francis of Assisi. But then God had given him at his birth the soul of a poet, as he himself when quite young had in mystical marriage taken poverty as his bride: and with the soul of a poet and the body of a beggar he found the way to perfection not difficult. He understood Christ, and so he became like him. We do not require the Liber Conformitatum to teach us that the life of St Francis was the true *Imitatio Christi*, a poem compared to which the book of that name is merely prose.

Indeed, that is the charm about Christ, when all is said: he is just like a work of art. He does not really teach one anything, but by being brought into his presence one becomes something. And everyone is predestined to his presence. Once at least in his life each man walks with Christ to Emmaus.

6 October

WILLIAM TYNDALE

TRANSLATOR, TEACHER AND REFORMATION
MARTYR, 1536

———◄○►———

From Tyndale's *Doctrinal Treatises*

Edited for the Parker Society by Henry Walter, 1848

Tyndale's version of the New Testament reached England in 1526. Opposition from the hierarchy had forced him to flee his native country, and he undertook the work of translation in Cologne, then at Worms. His robust and vital rendering into English, for which he argues so eloquently below, became the basis for both the Authorized Version and the Revised Version of the Bible. He never returned to England, and was arrested and burned at the stake in 1536, at Vilvorde, near Brussels.

The sermons which thou readest in the Acts of the apostles, and all that the apostles preached, were no doubt preached in the mother tongue. Why then might they not be written in the mother tongue? As if one of us preach a good sermon why may it not be written? Saint Jerome also translated the Bible into his mother tongue. Why may we not also? They will say it cannot be translated into our tongue it is so rude. It is not so rude as they are false liars. For the Greek tongue agreeth more with the English than with the Latin. And the properties of the Hebrew tongue agreeth a thousand times more with the English than with the Latin. The manner of speaking is both one, so that in a thousand places thou needest not but to translate it into English word for word, when thou must seek a compass in the Latin, and yet shall have much work to translate it well favouredly, so that it have the same grace and sweetness, sense and pure understanding with it in the Latin, and as it hath in the Hebrew. A thousand parts better may it be translated into the English, than into the Latin. Yea and except my memory fail me, and that I have forgotten what I read when I was a child, thou shalt find in the English chronicle how that King Adelstone (Athelstone) caused scripture to be translated into the tongue that then was in England, and how the prelates exhorted him thereto.

7 October

HENRY MELCHIOR MUHLENBERG

MISSIONARY TO AMERICA, 1787

———◄○►———

The Old Lutheran Bells at Home

Wallace Stevens, American, 1879–1955

As a great voice of American poetry, born in Pennsylvania where Muhlenberg did so much to establish the Lutheran church, Wallace Stevens' enigmatic verse acknowledges the venerable, generous and pastoral presence of Lutheranism in the East Coast society he knows as home (the voices of the pastors), while also acknowledging that every church has other voices equally strong though maybe less immediately distinct, with their own particular insights and limitations and vested interests to be asserted and maintained.

> These are the voices of the pastors calling
> In the names of St Paul and of the halo-John
> And of other holy and learned men, among them
>
> Great choristers, propounders of hymns, trumpeters,
> Jerome and the scrupulous Francis and Sunday women,
> The nurses of the spirit's innocence.
>
> These are the voices of the pastors calling
> Much rough-end being to smooth Paradise,
> Spreading out fortress walls like fortress wings.
>
> Deep in their sound the stentor Martin sings.
> Dark Juan looks outward through the mystic brow . . .
> Each sexton has his sect. The bells have none.

These are the voices of the pastors calling
And calling like the long echoes in long sleep,
Generations of shepherds to generations of sheep.

Each truth is a sect though no bells ring for it.
And the bells belong to the sextons, after all,
As they jangle and dangle and kick their feet.

THOMAS TRAHERNE*

PRIEST AND POET, 1674

———◄o►———

From *Centuries of Meditations*, II.66

Thomas Traherne, English, 1637–74

Traherne published very little work during his lifetime, and many of his manuscripts were not signed, so that they were lost until a chance purchase in 1896 led to the publication and widespread appreciation of some of Traherne's poems and the *Centuries*. Further unpublished manuscripts have been identified as recently as 1997. In her introduction to his selected works, the poet Anne Ridler says that Traherne is 'a master of the Affirmative Way, which pursues perfection through delight in the created world. Every emphasis in his writings is on inclusive love.' This excerpt from the *Centuries* (which keeps the author's idiosyncratic spelling) exemplifies what Ridler finds in Traherne's contemplative writing.

That violence wherwith som times a man doteth upon one Creature, is but a little spark of that lov, even towards all, which lurketh in His Nature. We are made to lov: both to satisfy the necessity of our Active Nature, and to answer the Beauties in evry Creature. By lov our souls are married and sodderd to the creatures: and it is our Duty like GOD to be united to them all. We must lov them infinitly but in God, and for God: and God in them: namely all His Excellencies Manifested in them. When we dote upon the Perfections and Beauties of som one Creature: we do not lov that too much, but other things too little. Never was any thing in this World loved too much, but many things have been loved in a fals Way: and all in too short a Measure.

Edith Cavell*
NURSE, 1915

———◄○►———

Two o'clock, the Morning of October 12th, 1915
Alice Meynell, English, 1847–1922

Set during the First World War, Meynell imagines the courage and dedication of Edith Cavell as she waits at dawn on the morning of her execution, having been sentenced to death for smuggling British soldiers to safety, and for refusing to implicate those who had worked with her. It is a time with which she is well accustomed as a nurse, and one which is far less frightening to her than for the sick whom she tended so carefully.

> To her accustomed eyes
> The midnight-morning brought not such a dread
> As thrills the chance-awakened head that lies
> In trivial sleep on the habitual bed.

> 'Twas yet some hours ere light;
> And many, many, many a break of day
> Had she outwatched the dying; but this night
> Shortened her vigil was, briefer the way.

> By dial of the clock
> 'Twas day in the dark above her lonely head.
> 'This day thou shalt be with Me.' Ere the cock
> Announced that day she met the Immortal Dead.

St Teresa of Avila*

TEACHER AND POET, 1582

———◄◦►———

From *The Flaming Heart*

Richard Crashaw, English, 1612–49

As foundress of the 'Discalced Carmelites' and writer on spiritual union
with God, Teresa of Avila (St Teresa of Jesus) is outstanding in that she
commends the contemplative life so powerfully both in her written works
and in the way she lived and enabled others to live. Here Crashaw, son of
Puritan parents and later convert to Roman Catholicism, celebrates both
Teresa and her teachings which he finds so compelling.

> O thou undaunted daughter of desires!
> By all thy dower of lights and fires;
> By all the eagle in thee, all the dove;
> By all thy lives and deaths of love;
> By thy large draughts of intellectual day,
> And by thy thirsts of love more large than they;
> By all thy brim-filled bowls of fierce desire,
> By thy last morning's draught of liquid fire;
> By the full kingdom of that final kiss
> That seized thy parting soul, and sealed thee his;
> By all the heavens thou hast in him
> (Fair sister of the Seraphim!);
> By all of him we have in thee;
> Leave nothing of myself in me.
> Let me so read thy life that I
> Unto all life of mine may die.

18 October

ST LUKE

EVANGELIST AND PHYSICIAN

———◄◦►———

The Word

Niyi Osundare, Nigerian, 1947–

Among the four Evangelists Luke stands out as the one who wrote a sequel to his Gospel, the Acts of the Apostles, which tells of how the Word of God in Christ is proclaimed through the ancient world, and how 'many of those who heard the word believed' (Acts 4.4). This African poem talks of how the Gospel disseminates, inspires, and gives rise to new vitality.

> *The Word*
> is a pod
> quick with unspoken seeds
> exploding in the dry season
> of occasion
>
> is an egg
> broken,
> it spreads
> ungatherably
> ear's food
> mind's nurture
> router of silences
> sun of noons of action

19 October

HENRY MARTYN*

TRANSLATOR AND MISSIONARY IN INDIA
AND PERSIA, 1812

———◦———

O Friend of my sad heart

From a hymn in Persian by Zand-i-Zol Qalam, Iranian,
translated by Norman Sharp

Christianity was well established in Iran by the second century, and sent
missionaries to the Far East, including China. Thus there are traces of
Christian influence in Persian poetry through the ages, some of which
arise from references in the Quran, and some from converts who were
drawn to the faith through the work of Western missionaries such as
Henry Martyn, who translated the Psalms and New Testament into
Persian. Here are three verses from a hymn written in the twentieth
century by an Iranian Christian, which Hassan Dehqani-Tafti, former
Anglican Bishop of Iran, describes as one of Persia's most beautiful.

O Friend of my sad heart, Thy kindness immense be!
   O Light of the world, may Thy presence intense be!
Whenever afflicted, with doubt or depression,
Whenever my helper neglects his profession,
Whenever it's hard to refrain from transgression,
   Draw near and relieve me, my Guardian hence be!

At length when my lifetime is nearing conclusion,
At length when all pleasure is tasteless intrusion,
At length when existence is changed to confusion,
   O changeless Preserver, my certain defence be!

No griefs or sore troubles can further distress me;
No tears shed in bitterness can still obsess me;
Now death has been vanquished, no dread can oppress me;
   Thou always within me the chief influence be!

26 October

ALFRED*

KING OF THE WEST SAXONS, AND SCHOLAR, 899

―――――◄◊►―――――

These are waterscapes that God had promised

From the Anglo-Saxon of King Alfred, ninth century,
translated by David Scott

Alfred is remembered not only as a just and wise ruler, but also as a scholar
who nourished the Church through his promotion of learning and spiritual devotion. He translated into Anglo-Saxon, or caused to be translated,
the Psalms and many books of the Bible, as well as important writings
from the early Church. In the preface to one of these texts, St Gregory's
Pastoral Rule, are poems, perhaps written by Alfred himself. One of these
celebrates the Holy Spirit who floods the hearts of the faithful.

> These are waterscapes that God had promised
> as a comfort to the world,
> He said that he would wish for evermore
> that living waters should flow into the world,
> from the hearts of all beneath the sky,
> that faithfully believe in him. There is little doubt
> these waterscapes their wellspring have
> in heaven, that is the Holy Ghost,
> from which the saints and chosen ones can draw.

26 October

PHILIPP NICOLAI, 1608;
JOHANN HEERMANN, 1647;
PAUL GERHARDT, 1676

HYMN WRITERS

———◄◦►———

The duteous day now closeth

Translated from German by Robert Bridges, English, 1844–1930

On this day the American Lutheran Calendar commemorates three of the great hymn writers and composers of tunes of German Protestantism: Philipp Nicolai (1556–1608), Johann Heermann (1585–1647) and Paul Gerhardt (1607–76). Their verses, many of which are translated into English, have continued to enrich Christian worship and personal piety in the Western Church through many generations. Gerhardt's exquisite evening hymn, translated from German by Robert Bridges for his *Yatten-don Hymnal* of 1895, exemplifies the depths of contemplative devotion to which these hymn writers give expression.

> The duteous day now closeth,
> Each flower and tree reposeth,
>   Shade creeps o'er wild and wood:
> Let us, as night is falling,
> On God our Maker calling,
>   Give thanks to him, the Giver good.

> Now all the heavenly splendour
> Breaks forth in starlight tender
>   From myriad worlds unknown;
> And man, the marvel seeing,
> Forgets his selfish being,
>   For joy of beauty not his own.

His care he drowneth yonder,
Lost in the abyss of wonder;
  To heaven his soul doth steal:
This life he disesteemeth,
The day it is that dreameth,
  That doth from truth his vision seal.

Awhile his mortal blindness
May miss God's lovingkindness,
  And grope in faithless strife:
But when life's day is over
Shall death's fair night discover
  The fields of everlasting life.

28 October

St Simon and St Jude
APOSTLES

———◄o►———

Salutation

Robert Herrick, English, 1591–1674

The Western churches celebrate the Apostles St Simon and St Jude as a pair, a reminder that mission is a shared witness from within the community of the Church (Luke 9.1ff.). This poem recalls the instructions Jesus gives to the 'seventy others' in Luke's Gospel (10.1ff.), whom he sends out ahead of him in pairs, that they should do nothing to hinder the task in hand. Herrick takes this concentrated focus in mission and ministry as the model for all who serve Christ – service which is not their own private project, but one in which they are graciously *sent*.

> Christ, I have read, did to His Chaplains say,
> Sending them forth, *Salute no man by th' way:*
> Not, that He taught His Ministers to be
> Unsmooth, or sowre, to all civilitie;
> But to instruct them, to avoid all snares
> Of tardination in the Lords Affaires.
> Manners are good: but till his errand ends,
> Salute we must, nor Strangers, Kin, or Friends.

31 October: Reformation Day
[CW Martin Luther, Reformer and Hymn Writer, 1546]

SAINTS AND MARTYRS OF THE REFORMATION ERA

———◀◦▶———

Thee will I love, my strength, my tower

Translated from the German of Johann Scheffler, 1624–77,
by John Wesley

These words by Johann Scheffler express the depth of spirituality which flourished in the late sixteenth and seventeenth centuries, both Catholic and Reformed, and which has formed Christian understanding ever since. Scheffler, known also as Angelus Silesius, was born the son of a Polish nobleman, grew up in the Christian faith as a Lutheran, and entered the Roman Catholic Church midway through his life, in 1653. While his theological work exhibits some of the fierce controversy of his time, his spiritual writing is steeped in the medieval German mystical tradition, and is deeply moving. Some of his poems were translated by John Wesley during his time in America, while minister of Savannah, 1735–7, where he learnt German.

Thee will I love, my strength, my tower;
  Thee will I love, my joy, my crown;
Thee will I love with all my power,
  In all my works, and thee alone!
Thee will I love till the pure fire
Fill my whole soul with chaste desire.

Ah! why did I so late thee know,
  Thee, lovelier than the sons of men!
Ah! why did I no sooner go
  To thee, the only ease in pain!
Ashamed I sigh, and inly mourn
That I so late to thee did turn.

In darkness willingly I stray'd;
    I sought thee, yet from thee I rov'd:
For wide my wandering thoughts were spread,
    Thy creatures more than thee I loved.
And now, if more at length I see,
'Tis through thy light, and comes from thee.

I thank thee, Uncreated Sun,
    That thy bright beams on me have shined;
I thank thee, who hast overthrown
    My foes, and heal'd my wounded mind;
I thank thee, whose enlivening voice
Bids my free heart in thee rejoice.

Uphold me, in the doubtful race,
    Nor suffer me again to stray;
Strengthen my feet, with steady pace
    Still to press forward in thy way;
My soul and flesh, O Lord of Might,
Fill, satiate with thy heavenly light.

Give to my eyes refreshing tears;
    Give to my heart chaste, hallow'd fires;
Give to my soul, with filial fears,
    The love that all heaven's host inspires:
'That all my powers, with all their might
In thy sole glory may unite.'

Thee will I love, my joy, my crown!
    Thee will I love, my Lord, my God!
Thee will I love, beneath thy frown
    Or smile, thy sceptre or thy rod.
What though my flesh and heart decay?
Thee shall I love in endless day!

8 November

SAINTS AND MARTYRS OF A NATION (OF ENGLAND AND WALES)*

━━◄◦►━━

I think continually of those who were truly great

Stephen Spender, English, 1909–95

In some provinces of the Anglican Communion this day is set aside for the remembrance of saints of the nation, or of the Communion itself. Spender's poem celebrates those who have gone before us and yet who remain as an inspiration in the manner of their living and their dying – a great cloud of witnesses.

I think continually of those who were truly great.
Who, from the womb, remembered the soul's history
Through corridors of light where the hours are suns
Endless and singing. Whose lovely ambition
Was that their lips, still touched with fire,
Should tell of the Spirit clothed from head to foot in song.
And who hoarded from the Spring branches
The desires falling across their bodies like blossoms.

What is precious is never to forget
The essential delight of the blood drawn from the ageless
    springs
Breaking through rocks in worlds before our earth.
Never to deny its pleasure in the simple morning light
Nor its grave evening demand for love.
Never to allow gradually the traffic to smother
With noise and fog the flowering of the spirit.

Near the snow, near the sun, in the highest fields
See how these names are fêted by the waving grass
And by the streamers of white cloud

And whispers of wind in the listening sky.
The names of those who in their lives fought for life
Who wore at their hearts the fire's centre.
Born of the sun they travelled a short while towards the
    sun,
And left the vivid air signed with their honour.

St Martin of Tours

BISHOP, *c*.397

————◄◦►————

From *St Martin and the Beggar*

Thom Gunn, Anglo-American, 1929–

This poem reflects on the nature of holiness demonstrated in the practical wisdom of Martin, the soldier-saint, who knows his own need as well as that of others. While travelling through the cold and wet, Martin encounters a beggar perishing in the bitter weather, and gives him half of his cloak – thus keeping them both alive.

> A ship that moves on darkness
> He rode across the plain,
> When a brawny beggar started up
> Who pulled at his rein
> And leant dripping with sweat and water
> Upon the horse's mane.
>
> He glared into Martin's eyes
> With eyes more wild than bold;
> His hair sent rivers down his spine;
> Like a fowl plucked to be sold
> His flesh was grey. Martin said –
> 'What, naked in this cold?
>
> 'I have no food to give you,
> Money would be a joke.'
> Pulling his new sword from the sheath
> He took his soldier's cloak
> And cut it in two equal parts
> With a single stroke.

Grabbing one to his shoulders,
Pinning it with his chin,
The beggar dived into the dark,
And soaking to the skin
Martin went on slowly
Until he reached the inn.

One candle on the wooden table,
The food and drink were poor,
The woman hobbled off, he ate,
Then casually before
The table stood the beggar as
If he had used the door.

Now dry for hair and flesh had been
By warm airs fanned,
Still bare but round each muscled thigh
A single golden band,
His eyes now wild with love, he held
The half cloak in his hand.

'You recognised the human need
Included yours, because
You did not hesitate, my saint,
To cut your cloak across;
But never since that moment
Did you regret the loss.

'My enemies would have turned away,
My holy toadies would
Have given all the cloak and frozen
Conscious that they were good.
But you, being a saint of men,
Gave only what you could.'

St Martin stretched his hand out
To offer from his plate,
But the beggar vanished, thinking food
Like cloaks is needless weight.
Pondering on the matter,
St Martin bent and ate.

144

SAMUEL SEABURY*
FIRST ANGLICAN BISHOP IN NORTH AMERICA,
1796

———◁◦▷———

Prayer

Christopher Jane Corkery, American, 1946–

Elected Bishop in the United States in 1783, Seabury was consecrated at Aberdeen in 1784, and his subsequent ministry secured a firm basis upon which the Episcopal Church in independent America could develop and flourish. Here is a poem by an American Christian yearning for the gift of prayer as the link that can hold together the exquisite beauty and the suffering of creation in a unity of wonder, compassion, and praise.

> Purge this one evil: tongue that utters nothing.
> Show me the word or else show me the dark
> where lightning seeds its next illicit sun.
> If it is love of you I haven't sung, if it is only war,
> then mark me down for hiding behind doors
> when Master Fear came calling. But then,
> between the pearling, jointless tide I saw at dawn
> and the cripple whose torqued spine breaks up this street,
> teach me the connection, silent, forging one.
> Shut my eyes. Pry my lips apart.

16 November

ST MARGARET OF SCOTLAND*

QUEEN OF SCOTLAND, PHILANTHROPIST AND
REFORMER OF THE CHURCH, 1093

———◆———

The spirit is too blunt an instrument

Anne Stevenson, Anglo-American, 1933–

An Anglo-Saxon princess who married Malcolm III of Scotland, Margaret stands out not only for her piety and service, but also as one of the few women saints who was a mother. In this poem, Anne Stevenson wonders at the child to whom she has given birth – a sheer miracle of biological process.

> The spirit is too blunt an instrument
> to have made this baby.
> Nothing so unskilful as human passions
> could have managed the intricate
> exacting particulars: the tiny
> blind bones with their manipulating tendons,
> the knee and the knucklebones, the resilient
> fine meshings of ganglia and vertebrae
> in the chain of the difficult spine.
>
> Observe the distinct eyelashes and sharp crescent
> fingernails, the shell-like complexity
> of the ear with its firm involutions
> concentric in miniature to the minute
> ossicles. Imagine the
> infinitesimal capillaries, the flawless connections
> of the lungs, the invisible neural filaments
> through which the completed body
> already answers to the brain.

Then name any passion or sentiment
possessed of the simplest accuracy.
No. No desire or affection could have done
with practice what habit
has done perfectly, indifferently,
through the body's ignorant precision.
It is left to the vagaries of the mind to invent
love and despair and anxiety
and their pain.

ELIZABETH OF HUNGARY
PRINCESS OF THURINGIA, AND PHILANTHROPIST, 1231

———◁◦▷———

Woman to Man

Judith Wright, Australian, 1915–2000

Daughter of the King of Hungary, Elizabeth married Louis IV, Landgrave of Thuringia, and enjoyed a happy relationship with him. Together they became parents of three children. After his death, Elizabeth devoted herself to a life of prayer and service of the poor.

The eyeless labourer in the night,
the selfless, shapeless seed I hold,
builds for its resurrection day –
silent and swift and deep from sight
foresees the unimagined light.

This is no child with a child's face;
this has no name to name it by:
yet you and I have known it well.
This is our hunter and our chase,
the third who lay in our embrace.

This is the strength that your arm knows,
the arc of flesh that is my breast,
the precise crystals of our eyes.
This is the blood's wild tree that grows
the intricate and folded rose.

This is the maker and the made;
this is the question and reply;
the blind head butting at the dark,
the blaze of light along the blade.
Oh hold me, for I am afraid.

ST HILDA*

ABBESS OF WHITBY, 680

————<◊>————

Caedmon's *Hymn*

From Bede's *Ecclesiastical History of the English People*, Book IV, 24, translated by Mark Pryce

Bede's *Ecclesiastical History* pays tribute to the significance of Hilda as a religious leader, and particularly to the great foundation of monks and nuns at Whitby over which she presided as Abbess. It was this abbey that the poet Caedmon entered once he had been given his miraculous creative gift, Bede says, and it was for Hilda and her community that he composed his verse. Bede tells the story of how Caedmon would leave the feast rather than take his turn in singing verse to the assembled company, until an angel comes to him in his lonely misery and bids him sing the praises of God the Creator. The *Hymn* which Caedmon sings occurs in Old English in some texts of Bede's *History*, and represents the birth of Christian religious poetry in English.

It sometimes happened that at a feast all the guests in turn would sing and entertain one another; then, when he saw the harp moving towards him, Cacdmon would leave the table and go home.

On one such occasion, having gone out of the house where the feast was being held to the stable where he had care of the cattle that night, he settled himself down to rest. Suddenly, one stood by him in his sleep and greeted him by name, saying: 'Caedmon, sing me a song.' But he answered 'I cannot sing, and because I cannot sing I left the banquet and came here.' Then the one who spoke replied 'Even so, you shall sing to me.' 'What shall I sing?' he asked. 'Sing the Creation of all things' the other replied. And immediately Caedmon began to sing the praise of God the Creator, singing verses which he had never heard before; a song like this:

We worship the Weaver of heaven's wide fabric,
majesty's Might, the Wisdom of minds,
creation's Keeper, Maker of marvels,
glory's Eternity, lordship's Life,
Who spread out space: for all creatures a canopy;
Who laid down the land as humanity's home.

MECHTILD OF MAGDEBURG*

MYSTIC, 1280

————◄◊►————

From *The Flowing Light of the Godhead*

These few lines from Mechtild's *Revelations* show the poetic sensibility with which she expressed the beauty of divine love for humanity unfolded to her in prayer.

> Love flows from God to humanity without effort
> As a bird glides·through the air
> Without moving its wings –
> Thus they go whithersoever they will
> United in body and soul
> Yet in their form separate –
>   As the Godhead strikes the note
> Humanity sings,
> The Holy Spirit is the harpist
> And all the strings must sound
> Which are strung in love.

22 November

St Cecilia*

MARTYR AT ROME AND PATRON OF MUSIC, *c.*230

————◄○►————

To Musick. A Song

Robert Herrick, English, 1591–1674

Though Cecilia was one of the most revered of the martyrs of the early Church, little is known of her beyond the apocryphal stories that she encouraged both her husband and her brother to become Christians. She is the patron saint of music and musicians.

> Musick, thou Queen of Heaven, Care-charming-spell,
>   That strik'st a stilnesse into hell:
> Thou that tam'st Tygers, and fierce storms that rise
>   With thy soule-melting Lullabies:
> Fall down, down, down, from those thy chiming spheres,
> To charme our soules, as thou enchant'st our eares.

ISAAC WATTS

HYMN WRITER, 1748

————◄◊►————

From *True Riches*

Isaac Watts, English, 1674–1748

One of the greatest of English hymn writers, Watts' verse still has an important place in the Church's worship, especially his Passion hymn, 'When I survey the wondrous cross'. These lines are grounded in an honest experience of praying, as they express both the richness of the contemplative, and the ever-present difficulties of distraction.

> I've a mighty Part within
> That the world hath never seen,
> Rich as *Eden*'s happy Ground,
> And with choicer Plenty crown'd.
> Here on all the shining Boughs
> Knowledge fair and useful grows;
> On the same young flow'ry Tree
> All the Seasons you may see;
> Notions in the Bloom of Light,
> Just disclosing to the Sight;
> Here are Thoughts of larger Growth,
> Rip'ning into solid Truth;
> Fruits refin'd, of noble Taste;
> Seraphs feed on such Repast.
> Here in green and shady Grove
> Streams of Pleasure mix with Love:
> There beneath the smiling Skies
> Hills of Contemplation rise;
> Now upon some shining Top
> Angels light, and call me up;
> I rejoice to raise my Feet,

Both rejoice when there we meet.
There are endless Beauties more
Earth hath no resemblance for;
Nothing like them round the Pole,
Nothing can describe the Soul:
'Tis a Region half unknown,
That hath Treasures of its own,
More remote from public View
Than the Bowels of *Peru*;
Broader 'tis and brighter far
Than the Golden *Indies* are;
Ships that trace the watry Stage
Cannot coast it in an Age;
Harts or Horses, strong and fleet,
Had they wings to help their Feet,
Could not run it half way o'er
In ten thousand Days and more.
Yet the silly wandring Mind
Loath to be too much confin'd
Roves and takes her daily Tours,
Coasting round the narrow Shores,
Narrow Shores of Flesh and Sense,
Picking Shells and Pebbles thence:
Or she sits at Fancy's Door,
Calling Shapes and Shadows to her,
Foreign Visits still receiving,
And t' her self a Stranger living.
Never, never would she buy
Indian Dust or *Tyrian* Dye,
Never trade abroad for more
If she saw her native Store,
If her inward Worth were known
She might ever live alone.

30 November

ST ANDREW

APOSTLE AND PATRON OF SCOTLAND

———◁◦▷———

From *Andreas*

Old English, *c.* late ninth century, translated by
Charles W. Kennedy

Patron of Scotland, Greece and Russia, Andrew appears in the Gospels as the brother of Peter, both of whom were fishermen called from their nets to join the mission of Jesus (Mark 1.16ff.). In the Anglican tradition, St Andrew's-tide is kept as a time of prayer for world mission. The Old English poem *Andreas* portrays Andrew as an heroic figure similar to Beowulf, who sails the ocean to rescue his fellow-apostle Matthew from prison, a narrative based on the apocryphal *Acts of Andrew and Matthew amongst the Anthropophagi*. In these lines from the poem, Andrew is on his voyage as the ship battles its way through a terrible storm. In the second part of the excerpt the sailor Andrew praises the skill of the ship's captain, unaware that the vessel has been piloted under the special protection of the almighty God.

The depths were troubled.   The horn-fish darted,
Gliding through ocean;   the gray gulls wheeled,
Searching for carrion.   The sun grew dark;
A gale arose,   and great waves broke;
The sea was stirred.   Halyards were humming,
Sails were drenched.   Sea-terror grew
In the welter of waves.   The thanes were adread,
Who sailed with Andrew   on the ocean-stream,
Nor hope with life   ever to come to land.
Not yet was it known   Who guided their bark
Through the breaking seas . . .
Sixteen voyages   early and late
It has been my lot   to sail in my sea-boat,

155

With freezing hands   as I smote the sea,
The ocean-streams.   Now this is another.
Never have I known   one like to thee,
Of the sons of men,   steering over stem.
The roaring billows   beat on the strand;
Full swift this bark   and most like a bird
Foamy-necked faring   over the waves.
Well I know   that I never have seen
In any sailor   more wondrous sea-craft.
Most like it is   as if on land
The boat stood still,   where wind and storm
Could stir it not,   nor breaking billows
Shatter the high prow;   yet it speeds over ocean
Swift under sail.

JOHN OF DAMASCUS*
THEOLOGIAN AND HYMN WRITER, *c.*749

————◁◦▷————

Thou hallowed chosen morn of praise

Translated from the Greek of John of Damascus
by John Mason Neale

John of Damascus' theological writings have been of great significance in churches of both East and West, particularly his summary of the teachings of the Greek Fathers, *De Fide Orthodoxa*. It is in praise, through the translations of his Easter hymns, that his theology has nourished the main body of believers. The hymns 'Come ye faithful, raise the strain' and 'The Day of Resurrection!' are well known; this hymn, with its exultant blend of scriptural image, corporate devotion and sacramental theology, less so.

Thou hallowed chosen morn of praise,
That best and greatest shinest:
Lady and queen and day of days,
Of things divine, divinest!
On thee our praises Christ adore
For ever and for evermore.

Come, let us taste the vine's new fruit,
For heavenly joy preparing;
To-day the branches with the Root
In Resurrection sharing:
Whom as true God our hymns adore
For ever and for evermore.

Rise, Sion, rise! and looking forth,
Behold thy children round thee!
From east and west, from south and north,
Thy scattered sons have found thee;

And in thy bosom Christ adore
For ever and for evermore.

O Father, O co-equal Son,
O co-eternal Spirit,
In persons Three, in substance One,
And One in power and merit;
In thee baptized, we thee adore
For ever and for evermore.

6 December

ST NICHOLAS

BISHOP OF MYRA, c.326

———◄○►———

Saint Nicholas

Marianne Moore, American, 1887–1972

Though patron of sailors and children, St Nicholas is more generally known as the bringer of gifts, Santa Claus (the American version of his name in Dutch – Sante Klaas). This poem is a wry meditation on desire, and on its narcissism and superficiality in a culture impoverished by consumerism, in which the commercial language of advertisement has possessed the imagination, so that what we hope to be given is at once impossible and synthetic, and where the 'adult' is both insatiable and self-centred.

> might I, if you can find it, be given
> a chameleon with tail
> that curls like a watch spring; and vertical
> on the body – including the face – pale
> tiger-stripes, about seven;
> (the melanin in the skin
> having been shaded from the sun by thin
> bars; the spiral dome
> beaded along the ridge
> as if it were platinum)?

> If you can find no striped chameleon,
> might I have a dress or a suit –
> I guess you have heard of it – of *qiviut*?
> and to wear with it, a taslon shirt, the drip-dry fruit
> of research second to none;
> sewn, I hope, by Excello;
> as for buttons to keep down the collar-points, no.

The shirt could be white –
and be 'worn before six',
either in daylight or at night.

But don't give me, if I can't have the dress,
a trip to Greenland, or grim
trip to the moon. The moon should come here. Let him
make the trip down, spread on my dark floor some dim
marvel, and if a success
that I stoop to pick up and wear,
I could ask nothing more. A thing yet more rare,
though, and different,
would be this: Hans von Marées'
St Hubert, kneeling with head bent,

erect – in velvet and tense with restraint –
hand hanging down: the horse, free.
Not the original, of course. Give me
a postcard of the scene – huntsman and divinity –
hunt-mad Hubert startled into a saint
by a stag with a Figure entined.
But why tell you what you must have divined?
Saint Nicholas, O Santa Claus,
would it not be the most
prized gift that ever was!

St Ambrose

BISHOP OF MILAN, TEACHER OF THE FAITH
AND HYMN WRITER, *c*.397

————◄◦►————

O splendour of God's glory bright

Translated from the Latin of St Ambrose by Robert Bridges,
English, 1844–1930

Ambrose was a fine teacher and preacher whose pioneering use of hymns
has shaped Christian worship in the Western Church. He had a profound
influence on St Augustine, who records the introduction of hymn singing
into the worship at Milan in his *Confessions* (9.7). Though the authorship
of only three hymns can be ascribed with certainty to Ambrose, of which
this morning hymn is one, his style set the pattern for subsequent Latin
hymn writers.

> O splendour of God's glory bright,
> O thou that bringest light from light,
> O Light of light, light's living spring,
> O Day, all days illumining.
>
> O thou true Sun, on us thy glance
> Let fall in royal radiance,
> The Spirit's sanctifying beam
> Upon our earthly senses stream.
>
> The Father, too, our prayers implore,
> Father of glory evermore;
> The Father of all grace and might,
> To banish sin from our delight:

To guide whate'er we nobly do,
With love all envy to subdue,
To make ill-fortune turn to fair,
And give us grace our wrongs to bear.

Our mind be in his keeping placed,
Our body true to him and chaste,
Where only faith her fire shall feed,
To burn the tares of Satan's seed.

And Christ to us for food shall be,
From him our drink that welleth free,
The Spirit's wine, that maketh whole,
And, mocking not, exalts the soul.

Rejoicing may this day go hence,
Like virgin dawn our innocence,
Like fiery noon our faith appear,
Nor know the gloom of twilight drear.

Morn in her rosy car is borne;
Let him come forth our perfect morn,
The Word in God the Father one,
The Father perfect in the Son.

All laud to God the Father be,
All praise, eternal Son, to thee;
All glory, as is ever meet,
To God the holy Paraclete.

8 December

THE CONCEPTION OF THE
BLESSED VIRGIN MARY*

———◄◦►———

From *The Blessed Virgin Compared to the Air We Breathe*

Gerard Manley Hopkins, English, 1844–89

Though the tradition of the sinlessness of Mary, Mother of the Lord, has an ancient history in Eastern and Western Christianity, as does the celebration of her conception, as a doctrine the Immaculate Conception was defined by the Roman Catholic Church only as late as 1854, during Hopkins' lifetime. In this poem he celebrates the grace of God which embraces us all in Christ – 'I say that we are wound/With mercy round and round/As if with air', but which is especially present in the life of his mother – 'the same/Is Mary, more by name'.

> Wild air, world-mothering air,
> Nestling me everywhere,
> That each eyelash or hair
> Girdles; goes home betwixt
> The fleeciest, frailest-flixed
> Snowflake; that's fairly mixed
> With, riddles, and is rife
> In every least thing's life;
> This needful, never spent,
> And nursing element;
> My more than meat and drink,
> My meal at every wink;
> This air, which, by life's law,
> My lung must draw and draw
> Now but to breathe its praise,
> Minds me in many ways
> Of her who not only

Gave God's infinity
Dwindled to infancy
Welcome in the womb and breast,
Birth, milk, and all the rest
But mothers each new grace
That does now reach our race –
Mary Immaculate,
Merely a woman, yet
Whose presence, power is
Great as no goddess's
Was deemèd, dreamèd; who
This one work has to do –
Let all God's glory through,
God's glory which would go
Through her and from her flow
Off, and no way but so.

13 December

SAMUEL JOHNSON*

WRITER, MORALIST AND SCHOLAR, 1784

———◄○►———

From *The Rambler*, No. 17

Author, lexicographer and conversationalist, Johnson was a devout Christian and serious Anglican. He wrote many sermons, and his twice-weekly essays known as *The Rambler* (1750–2) earned him the title of 'the Great Moralist'. In this excerpt Johnson writes of the life-enhancing perspective that a frequent contemplation of death may give – a suitably Advent theme – particularly in combating the distorting sin of envy, and lessening the pain of grief at the loss of status or possession, or even the loss of loved ones.

He that considers how soon he must close his life will find nothing of so much importance than to close it well; and will, therefore, look with indifference to whatever is useless to that purpose. Whoever reflects frequently upon the uncertainty of his own duration, will easily find out, that the state of others is not more permanent; and that what can confer nothing on himself very desirable, cannot so much improve the condition of a rival, as to make him, in any great degree, superior to those from whom he has carried the prize, a prize too mean to excite a very obstinate opposition.

Even grief, that passion to which the virtuous and tender mind is more particularly subject, will be obviated, or alleviated, by the same reflection. It will be obviated, if all the blessings of our condition are enjoyed with a constant sense of the uncertain tenure by which they are held: if we remember, that whatever we possess is to be in our hands a very little time, and that the little, which our most lively hopes can promise us, may be made less, by ten thousand accidents, we shall not much repine at a loss, of which we cannot estimate the value, but of which, though we cannot tell the least amount, we know, with sufficient certainty, the greatest; and are convinced that the greatest is not much to be regretted.

But if any passion has so much usurped our understanding, as not to suffer us to enjoy our advantages with the moderation prescribed by reason and virtue, it is not too late to apply this remedy, when we find ourselves sinking under sorrow, and inclined to pine for that which is irrecoverably vanished. We may then usefully resolve the uncertainty of our own condition, and the folly of lamenting that from which, if it had stayed a little longer, we should ourselves have been taken away.

With regard to the sharpest and most melting sorrow, that which arises from the loss of those we have loved with tenderness, it may be observed that friendship between mortals can be contracted on no other terms, than that one must sometime mourn for the other's death: and this grief will always yield to the survivor one consolation proportionate to his affliction; for the pain, whatever it be, that he himself feels, his friend has escaped.

St John of the Cross

POET AND TEACHER, 1591

———◄◦►———

With a Divine Intention

St John of the Cross, translated from the Spanish by
Roy Campbell, South African, 1901–57

St John's principal work is *The Spiritual Canticle*, first published in 1627.
Other poems, such as this, mostly written in the Spanish ballad metre, also
tell of mystical encounter with God and of the experience of divine love.

> Without support, yet well supported,
> Though in pitch-darkness, with no ray,
> Entirely I am burned away.
>
> My spirit is so freed from every
> Created thing, that through the skies,
> Above herself, she's lifted, flies,
> And as in a most fragrant reverie,
> Only on God her weight applies.
> The thing which most my faith esteems
> For this one fact will be reported –
> Because my soul above me streams
> Without support, yet well supported.
>
> What though I languish in the shades
> As through my mortal life I go,
> Not over-heavy is my woe,
> Since if no glow my gloom invades,
> With a celestial life I glow.
> The love of such a life, I say,
> The more benightedly it darkens,
> Turns more to that to which it hearkens,
> Though in pitch-darkness, with no ray.

Since I knew Love, I have been taught
He can perform most wondrous labours.
Though good and bad in me are neighbours
He turns their difference to naught
Then both into Himself, so sweetly,
And with a flame so fine and fragrant
Which now I feel in me completely
Reduce my being, till no vagrant
Vestige of my own self can stay.
And wholly I am burned away.

CHRISTMAS EVE*

————◁◦▷————

Nativity

John Donne, English, 1572–1631

This sonnet on Christmas and Epiphany is from *La Corona*, the third of a series of seven devotional poems which Donne composed on the life, death, resurrection and ascension of Christ, as a 'crown of prayer and praise'.

> *Immensity cloistered in thy dear womb,*
> Now leaves his well-beloved imprisonment,
> There he hath made himself to his intent
> Weak enough, now into our world to come;
> But oh, for thee, for him, hath th'inn no room?
> Yet lay him in this stall, and from the orient,
> Stars, and wisemen will travel to prevent
> Th'effect of Herod's jealous general doom.
> See'st thou, my soul, with thy faith's eyes, how he
> Which fills all place, yet none holds him, doth lie?
> Was not his pity towards thee wondrous high,
> That would have need to be pitied by thee?
> Kiss him, and with him into Egypt go,
> *With his kind mother, who partakes thy woe.*

26 December

ST STEPHEN

DEACON AND FIRST MARTYR

———◦———

Jerusalem

James Fenton, English, 1949–

In the city which rejected the prophets, over which Jesus wept and in which he was crucified, Stephen becomes the first to witness to the Lord by his death. In this striking poem James Fenton captures the terrible dynamic of the Holy City still divided and at war within itself as the bitter history of religious intolerance and territorial rivalry recurs in the daily lives of its citizens.

I   Stone cries to stone,
         Heart to heart, heart to stone,
    And the interrogation will not die
        For there is no eternal city
        And there is no pity
    And there is nothing underneath the sky
        No rainbow and no guarantee –
    There is no covenant between your God and me.

II   It is superb in the air.
         Suffering is everywhere
    And each man wears his suffering like a skin.
        My history is proud.
        Mine is not allowed.
    This is the cistern where all wars begin,
        The laughter from the armoured car.
    This is the man who won't believe you're what you
         are.

III   This is your fault.
          This is a crusader vault.
   The Brook of Kidron flows from Mea She'arim.
      I will pray for you.
      I will tell you what to do.
 I'll stone you. I shall break your every limb.
      Oh I am not afraid of you
But maybe I should fear the things you make me do.

IV   This is not Golgotha.
       This is the Holy Sepulchre,
The Emperor Hadrian's temple to a love
     Which he did not much share.
     Golgotha could be anywhere.
Jerusalem itself is on the move.
     It leaps and leaps from every hill
And as it makes its way it also makes its will.

V   The city was sacked.
      Jordan was driven back.
The pious Christians burned the Jews alive.
     This is a minaret.
     I'm not finished yet.
We're waiting for reinforcements to arrive.
     Was that your mother's real name?
Would it be safe today to go to Bethlehem?

VI   This is the Garden Tomb.
      No, this is the Garden Tomb.
I'm an Armenian. I am a Copt.
     This is Utopia.
     I came here from Ethiopia.
This hole is where the flying carpet dropped
     The Prophet off to pray one night
And from here one hour later he resumed his flight.

VII   Who packed your bag?
          I packed my bag.
    Where was your uncle's mother's sister born?
          Have you ever met an Arab?
          Yes I am a scarab.
    I am a worm. I am a thing of scorn.
          I cry Impure from street to street
    And see my degradation in the eyes I meet.

VIII   I am your enemy.
          This is Gethsemane.
    The broken graves look to the Temple Mount.
          Tell me now, tell me when
          When shall we all rise again?
    Shall I be first in that great body count?
          When shall the tribes be gathered in?
    When, tell me, when shall the Last Things begin?

IX   You are in error.
          This is terror.
    This is your banishment. This land is mine.
          This is what you earn.
          This is the land of No Return.
    This is our sour dough, this the sweet wine.
          This is my history, this my race
    And this unhappy man threw acid in my face.

X   Stone cries to stone,
          Heart to heart, heart to stone.
    These are the warrior archaeologists.
          This is us and that is them.
          This is Jerusalem.
    These are the dying men with tattooed wrists.
          Do this and I'll destroy your home.
    I have destroyed your home. You have destroyed
          my home.

27 December

St John

APOSTLE AND EVANGELIST

———◄○►———

From *A Death in the Desert*

Robert Browning, English, 1812–89

Browning imagines the writer of Revelation, John the Beloved Disciple, reflecting on his mission and ministry as an evangelist and teacher as he draws towards the end of his long life, the only one of Christ's Apostles remaining (see John 21.20ff.). He wonders how people will come to believe in future generations, and trusts that the Gospel account will give definite shape to the mysteries of Christ's death and resurrection and abiding presence, which seem so distant in time, and yet are ever-present spiritual realities for those who have faith. This long poem was first published in 1864, at a time when critical studies began to challenge received notions about Scripture and its witness to Jesus as an historical figure.

'If I live yet, it is for good, more love
Through me to men: be nought but ashes here
That keep awhile my semblance, who was John, –
Still, when they scatter, there is left on earth
No one on earth who knew (consider this!)
– Saw with his eyes and handled with his hands
That which was from the first, the Word of Life.
How will it be when none more saith "I saw"?

'Such ever was love's way: to rise, it stoops.
Since I, whom Christ's mouth taught, was bidden teach,
I went, for many years, about the world,
Saying "It was so; so I heard and saw,"
Speaking as the case asked: and men believed.
Afterward came the message to myself
In Patmos isle; I was not bidden teach,

173

But simply listen, take a book and write,
Nor set down other than the given word,
With nothing left to my arbitrament
To choose or change: I wrote, and men believed.
Then, for my time grew brief, no message more,
No call to write again, I found a way,
And, reasoning from my knowledge, merely taught
Men should, for love's sake, in love's strength believe;
Or I would pen a letter to a friend
And urge the same as friend, nor less nor more:
Friends said I reasoned rightly, and believed.
But at the last, why, I seemed left alive
Like a sea-jelly weak on Patmos strand,
To tell dry sea-beach gazers how I fared
When there was mid-sea, and the mighty things;
Left to repeat, "I saw, I heard, I knew,"
And go all over the old ground again,
With Antichrist already in the world,
And many Antichrists, who answered prompt
"Am I not Jasper as thyself art John?
Nay, young, whereas through age thou mayest forget:
Wherefore, explain, or how shall we believe?" . . .

'And how shall I assure them? Can they share
– They, who have flesh, a veil of youth and strength
About each spirit, that needs must bide its time,
Living and learning still as years assist
Which wear the thickness thin, and let man see –
With me who hardly am withheld at all,
But shudderingly, scarce a shred between,
Lie bare to the universal prick of light?
It is for nothing we grow old and weak,
We whom God loves? When pain ends, gain ends too.
To me, that story – ay, that Life and Death
Of which I wrote "it was" – to me, it is;
– Is, here and now: I apprehend nought else.
Is not God now i' the world His power first made?

174

Is not His love at issue still with sin
Visibly when a wrong is done on earth?
Love, wrong, and pain, what see I else around?
Yea, and the Resurrection and Uprise
To the right hand of the throne – what is it beside,
When such truth, breaking bounds, o'erfloods my soul,
And, as I saw the sin and death, even so
See I the need yet transiency of both,
The good and glory consummated thence?
I saw the power; I see the Love, once weak,
Resume the power; and in this word "I see,"
Lo, there is recognized the Spirit of both
That moving o'er the spirit of man, unblinds
His eye and bids them look. These are, I see;
But ye, the children, His beloved ones too,
Ye need, – as I should use an optic glass
I wondered at erewhile, somewhere I' the world,
It had been given a crafty smith to make;
A tube, he turned on objects brought too close,
Lying confusedly insubordinate
For the unassisted eye to master once:
Look through his tube, at distance now they lay,
Become succinct, distinct, so small, so clear!
Just thus, ye needs must apprehend what truth
I see, reduced to plain historic fact,
Diminished into clearness, proved a point
And far away: ye would withdraw your sense
From out eternity, strain it upon time,
Then stand before the fact, that Life and Death,
Stay there at gaze, till it disport, dispread,
As though a star should open out, all sides,
Grow the world on you, as it is my world.'

28 December

THE HOLY INNOCENTS

———◄◊►———

Innocent's Song

Charles Causley, English, 1917–

In this ironic verse 'the Innocent' is the voice of the poet wondering in consternation at the seemingly harmless yet sinister 'smiling stranger' who has made his way into the home to disturb its domestic bliss. This King of greed and power comes at Christmas time disguised as an alluring 'Innocent' – to kill innocence. For he is the fanatical terrorist; he exploits sexuality and destructive materialism – the beguiling slayer of children.

> Who's that knocking on the window,
> Who's that standing at the door,
> What are all those presents
> Lying on the kitchen floor?
>
> Who is the smiling stranger
> With hair as white as gin,
> What is he doing with the children
> And who could have let him in?
>
> Why has he rubies on his fingers,
> A cold, cold crown on his head,
> Why, when he caws his carol,
> Does the salty snow run red?
>
> Why does he ferry my fireside
> As a spider on a thread,
> His fingers made of fuses
> And his tongue of gingerbread?

Why does the world before him
Melt in a million suns,
Why do his yellow, yearning eyes
Burn like saffron buns?

Watch where he comes walking
Out of the Christmas flame,
Dancing, double-talking:

Herod is his name.

Sources and Acknowledgements

Abelard, Peter, 'O what their joy and their glory must be', trans. John Mason Neale, *The English Hymnal*, Oxford University Press, 1933.

Alcuin of York, 'Whoever stole you from that bush of broom', trans. Helen Waddell, *Medieval Latin Lyrics*, Penguin, 1952.

Alfred, 'These are the waterscapes that God had promised', trans. David Scott, from *Ink and Spirit: Literature and Spirituality*, ed. Stephen Platten, Canterbury Press, 2000.

Ambrose of Milan, 'O splendour of God's glory bright', trans. Robert Bridges, *The English Hymnal*, Oxford University Press, 1933.

'Andreas', trans. Charles W. Kennedy, *The Earliest English Poetry: A Critical Survey*, Oxford University Press, 1943.

Augustine of Hippo, *Confessions*, trans. Henry Chadwick, Oxford University Press, 1991.

Baxter, Richard, 'He wants not friends that hath thy love', *The English Hymnal*, Oxford University Press, 1933.

Bede, 'Death Song', from Cuthbert's letter on the illness and death of the Venerable Bede, trans. Mark Pryce, 2002.

Bonhoeffer, Dietrich, 'Powers of Good', *Letters and Papers from Prison*, ed. Eberhard Bethge, enlarged edn, SCM Press, 1971.

Bridges, Robert, 'Laus Deo', *The Poetical Works of Robert Bridges*, ed. Geoffrey Keynes, Faber & Faber, 1946.

Brooke, Rupert, 'The Song of the Pilgrims', *The Poetical Works of Rupert Brooke*, ed. Geoffrey Keynes, Faber & Faber, 1946.

Browning, Robert, 'A Death in the Desert', *Robert Browning: A Critical Edition of the Major Works*, Oxford University Press, 1997.

Bseiso, Mu'een, 'The Vinegar Cup', *Anthology of Modern Palestinian Literature*, ed. Salma Khadra Jayyusi, Columbia University Press, New York, 1992.

Bunyan, John, *The Pilgrim's Progress*, from the facsimile edition, Unwin Brothers, Old Woking, 1978.

Caedmon, 'Hymn to the Creator' from Bede's *Ecclesiastical History of the English People*, Book IV, Chapter 24, trans. Mark Pryce, 2002.

Carmina Gadelica, trans. Alexander Carmichael, 1900.

Causley, Charles, 'Innocent's Song', *Collected Poems 1951–97*, Macmillan, 1992.

Clare of Assisi, 'First Letter to Blessed Agnes of Prague', from *Francis and Clare: the Complete Works*, trans. Regis J. Armstrong and Ignatius C. Brady, Paulist Press, 1982. Used with permission of Paulist Press.

Coleridge, Samuel Taylor, 'In looking at objects of Nature', from the *Notebooks*, given in *From Darkness to Light: a Confession of Faith in the Form of an Anthology*, ed. Victor Gollancz, Gollancz, 1956.

Corkery, Christopher Jane, 'Prayer', *Blessing*, Princeton University Press, 1985.

Cranmer, Thomas, Preface to *The Book of Common Prayer*, 1662.

Crashaw, Richard, 'The Flaming Heart', from *The Faber Book of Religious Verse*, ed. Helen Gardner, Faber, 1972.

Dickinson, Emily, 'A thought went up my mind to-day', given in *From Darkness to Light: a Confession of Faith in the Form of an Anthology*, ed. Victor Gollancz, Gollancz, 1956.

Donne, John, 'Love's Growth', 'Nativity', *John Donne: the Complete English Poems*, Penguin, 1971.

Dryden, John, 'Hymn for the Nativity of St John Baptist', *Poems*, ed. J. Sergaunt, Oxford University Press, 1945.

Eliot, George, 'O may I join the choir invisible', *Selected Essays, Poems and Other Writings*, ed. A. S. Byatt, Penguin, 1990.

Endo, Shusaku, *A Life of Jesus*, trans. Richard A. Schuchert, Paulist Press, New York, 1978.

Fenton, James, 'Jerusalem', *Out of Danger*, Penguin, 1993. Reprinted by permission of Peters Fraser and Dunlop on behalf of James Fenton.

Fortunatus, Venantius, 'Vexilla Regis', trans. John Mason Neale, *The English Hymnal*, Oxford University Press, 1933.

Franck, Johannes, 'Deck thyself, my soul, with gladness', trans. Catherine Winkworth, *The English Hymnal*, Oxford University Press, 1933.

Gascoyne, David, 'September Sun: 1947', reprinted from *Collected Poems: 1988* by permission of Oxford University Press.

Gerhardt, Paul, 'The duteous day now closeth', trans. Robert Bridges, *The English Hymnal*, Oxford University Press, 1933.

Gregory of Nazianzus, 'Hymn to God', *Selected Poems*, trans. John McGuckin, SLG Press, Oxford, 1995.

Grundtvig, Nikolai, 'Lord, from you we cannot flee', trans. Kenneth Stevenson, *Handing On: Borderlands of Worship and Tradition*, Darton, Longman and Todd, 1996.

Gunn, Thom, 'St Martin and the Beggar', *The Sense of Movement*, Faber & Faber, 1957.

Hammarskjöld, Dag, 'The moon was caught in the branches', *Markings*, trans. Leif Sjöberg and W. H. Auden, Faber & Faber, 1964.

Havel, Vaclav, 'A Word About Words', *Open Letters*, trans. Paul Wilson, Faber, 1991.

Herbert, George, 'Prayer', *The Complete English Works*, Everyman, 1974.

Herrick, Robert, 'Beginnings and Endings', 'To Musick. A song', 'Salutation', *Poems*, ed. L. C. Martin, Oxford University Press, 1965.

Hopkins, Gerard Manley, 'The Blessed Virgin Compared to the Air We Breathe', *Poems*, ed. Robert Bridges, Oxford University Press, 1930.

Jennings, Elizabeth, 'A View of Lazarus', *Praises*, Carcanet, Manchester, 1998.

John of the Cross, 'With a Divine Intention', trans. Roy Campbell, *Collected Poems of Roy Campbell*, Volume III, The Bodley Head, 1960.

John of Damascus, 'Thou hallowed chosen morn of praise', trans. John Mason Neale, *The English Hymnal*, Oxford University Press, 1933.

Johnson, Samuel, *The Rambler*, 17, 1750.

Keble, John, 'Morning', *The Christian Year: Thoughts in Verse for the Sundays and Holydays throughout the Year*, 1827.

Ken, Thomas, 'Her Virgin eyes saw God incarnate born', from *The English Hymnal*, Oxford University Press, 1933.

King, Martin Luther, 'Transformed Nonconformist', *Strength to Love*, 1963; Collins Fount, 1982.

Law, William, *The Absolute Unlawfulness of the Stage Entertainment, Fully Demonstrated*. 1726.

Lawrence, D. H., 'Pax', *Last Poems*, Heinemann, 1964.

Lewis, Saunders, 'Saint David's Last Sermon', *Selected Poems*, trans. Joseph P. Clancy, University of Wales Press, Cardiff, 1993.

Luther, Martin, 'From deepest woe I cry to thee', trans. Catherine Winkworth, *The Hymnal 1982*, Church Hymnal Corporation, New York.

MacCaig, Norman, 'True Ways of Knowing', *Collected Poems*, Chatto & Windus, 1990, used by permission of the Random House Group Ltd.

MacDonald, Ann, 'Soul-Shrine', *Of Women and Angels: the Virago Book of Spirituality*, ed. Sarah Anderson, Virago, 1996.

Mason, Anita, *The Illusionist*, Hamish Hamilton, 1983.

Mechtild of Magdeburg, 'The Flowing Light of the Godhead', extract published in *Of Women and Angels: the Virago Book of Spirituality*, ed. Sarah Anderson, Virago, 1996.

Merton, Thomas, 'Clairvaux', 'Two Desert Fathers', *Collected Poems*, New Directions, New York, 1980; reprinted by permission of New Directions.

Meynell, Alice, 'Two o'clock, the Morning of October 12th, 1915', *Complete Poems*, Burns Oates & Washbourne, 1923.

Milton, John, 'On His Blindness', 'At a Solemn Musick', *Complete English Poems*, Everyman, 1990.

Moore, Marianne, 'What Are Years?', 'Saint Nicholas', *Complete Poems*, Macmillan/Viking, New York, 1981. 'Saint Nicholas', copyright © 1958 by Marianne Moore, renewed from *The Complete Poems of Marianne Moore* by Marianne Moore. Used by permission of Viking Penguin, a division of Penguin Putnam Inc.

More, Thomas, 'Eye-flattering fortune', given in Anthony Kenny, *Thomas More*, Oxford University Press, 1983 (Past Masters series).

Murray, Les, 'Visitor', 'The Pay for Fosterage', 'The Meaning of Existence', *Poems the Size of Photographs*, Carcanet, 2002.

Newman, John Henry, *Apologia pro Vita Sua*, 1873.

Ntiru, Richard, 'If it is true', from *Penguin Book of African Poetry*, Penguin, 1998.

Osundare, Niyi, 'The Word', *Selected Poems*, Heinemann, 1992; reprinted by permission of Heinemann, part of Harcourt Education Ltd.

Parker, Dorothy, 'Paging St Patrick', *Complete Poems*, Penguin, 1999.

Qalam, Zand-i-Zol, 'O Friend of my sad heart', trans. Norman Sharp, from H. B. Dehqani-Tafti, *Christ and Christianity in Persian Poetry*, Sohrab Books, Basingstoke, 1986.

Raine, Kathleen, 'The Holy Isles', 'Peace of Mind', *Selected Poems*, Golgonooza Press, Ipswich, 1988; *The Inner Journey of the Poet and Other Papers*, ed. Brian Keeble, Allen & Unwin, 1982.

Rolle, Richard, 'Prayer before, during and after food', *The Form of Living*, trans. Mark Pryce.

Rossetti, Christina, 'St Peter', 'Up-hill', *Poetical Works*, Macmillan, 1914; 'A life of hope deferred', 'Darkness and light', *Time Flies: a Reading Diary*, SPCK, 1897.

Sahi, Jane, 'He could not be hidden', from Eric Lott, *Healing Wings: Acts of Jesus for Human Wholeness*, Asian Trading Corporation, Bangalore, 1998.

Scheffler, Johann, 'Thee will I love, my strength, my tower', trans. John Wesley, from *John and Charles Wesley: Selected Writings and Hymns*, ed. Frank Whaling, Paulist Press/SPCK, 1981.

Sitwell, Edith, *Selected Letters*, ed. J. Lehman and D. Parker, Macmillan, 1970; *Taken Care Of: the Autobiography*, Atheneum, New York, 1965.

Smith, Stevie, 'The Airy Christ', copyright © 1972, reprinted by permission of the New Directions Publishing Corporation and the Estate of James MacGibbon.

Spender, Stephen, 'I think continually of those who were truly great', *Poems*, Faber & Faber, 1933.

Stevens, Wallace, 'The Old Lutheran Bells at Home', *Collected Poems of Wallace Stevens*, Vintage Books, New York, 1990; reprinted with permission of Random House Inc.

Stevenson, Anne, 'The spirit is too blunt an instrument', *Selected Poems 1956–1986*, Oxford University Press, 1989.

Studdert Kennedy, Geoffrey, 'Waste', *The Sorrows of God and Other Poems*, Hodder & Stoughton, 1921.

Taylor, Jeremy, 'A cheerful spirit', *XXV Sermons*, 1653.

Tegner, Esaias, 'The Children of the Lord's Supper', trans. Henry Longfellow, *The Complete Works of Henry W. Longfellow*, Collins, n.d.

Tennyson, Alfred, 'Come, when no graver cares employ', *Poems*, Cassell, 1905.

183

Thomas, R. S., 'Reward', *Residues*, ed. M. Wynn Thomas, Bloodaxe Books, 2002.

Traherne, Thomas, 'Churches', *Poems, Centuries and Three Thanksgivings*, ed. Anne Ridler, Oxford University Press, 1966.

Trollope, Anthony, *Barchester Towers*, 1857; Penguin, 1994.

Tyndale, William, *Doctrinal Treatises* (1848); ed. Henry Walter, Parker Society.

Underhill, Evelyn, 'Divine Ignorance', *Theophanies*, Dent, 1926.

Vaughan, Henry, 'Peace', *Poetry and Selected Prose*, Oxford University Press, 1963.

Walcott, Derek, 'The Muse of History', from *Is Massa Day Dead?*, ed. O. Coombs, Doubleday-Anchor, New York, 1974.

Watkins, Vernon, 'Injustice and Praise', *Collected Poems*, Golgonooza Press, Ipswich, 2000.

Watts, Isaac, 'True Riches', from *All the Days of My Life*, ed. Philip Davis, J. M. Dent, 1999.

Waugh, Evelyn, *Helena*, Penguin, 1983.

Wesley, Charles, 'Thou Shepherd of Israel, and mine', 1780 Hymnbook, from *John and Charles Wesley: Selected Writings and Hymns*, ed. Frank Whaling, Paulist Press/SPCK, 1981.

Wesley, John, Preface to the 1780 Hymnbook, from *John and Charles Wesley: Selected Writings and Hymns*, ed. Frank Whaling, Paulist Press/SPCK, 1981.

Wilde, Oscar, 'De Profundis' (1897), *Selected Works*, ed. Richard Aldington, Heinemann, 1947.

Wright, Judith, 'Grace', 'Woman to Man', *A Human Pattern: Selected Poems 1942–1985*, ETT Imprint, Sydney, 1996.

Yeats, W. B., 'He Wishes for the Cloths of Heaven', from *The Wind Among the Reeds* (1899), in *Selected Poetry*, Macmillan, 1974.

INDEX OF
AUTHORS AND TRANSLATORS

INDEX OF FIRST LINES